ESSEX
Teashop Walks

Other areas covered in the *Teashop Walks* series include:

ESSEX

Teashop Walks

Ann and Norman Skinner

COUNTRYSIDE BOOKS
NEWBURY BERKSHIRE

COUNTRYSIDE BOOKS
3 Catherine Road
Newbury, Berkshire

To view our complete range of books,
please visit us at
www.countrysidebooks.co.uk

ISBN 1 85306 684 2

Designed by Graham Whiteman
Cover illustration by Colin Doggett
Photographs by Ann Skinner
Maps by the authors and redrawn by Jennie Collins

Produced through MRM Associates Ltd., Reading
Typeset by Techniset Typesetters, Newton-le-Willows
Printed by Woolnough Bookbinding Ltd., Irthlingborough

Contents

Walk

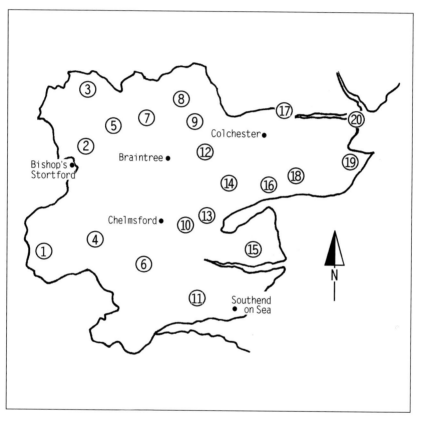

Area map showing the locations of the walks.

Introduction

It was with great excitement and a little trepidation that we stepped into a little known world to research and write a book about walks from teashops. Within the first few visits we were more than delighted to discover a whole new network of establishments that could assist in our enjoyment of both walks and visits to the far flung corners of Essex.

We are both great fans of BBC Essex and have appeared on *Tea at Three*. Why this proud boast you are asking? It is the words of their introduction song that ring in our ears. They seem so appropriate to this undertaking. Speaking of a cup of tea the lyrics run as follows: 'Yes it's a very good English custom, It's a stimulant for the brain, When you feel a little weary, a cup'll make you cheery and it's cheaper than Champagne!'

Having drawn up a guide list of places we really wanted to either visit for the first time, or go back to and have a further look, the detailed research began. We regret we were in fact only able to choose 20 because the original list was twice this. We had not considered a luncheon visit to anywhere other than a pub since the dim distant years when the children had to be catered for. How things have changed in the passing years. We found many old buildings pressed into second millennium use as a teashop, enabling members of the public to see inside properties that would not otherwise be open to them. We found many smart, well run businesses driven by a sense of service to the public. We soon became experts at choosing light bites and an interesting range of drinks to go with them.

We have tried to give you a flavour of each establishment and provide a quick guide so you can see why we are so attracted to each of them. Teashops are even more variable in character than pubs. There are those who take pride in the range of teas from the traditional to those hitherto unheard of. Some shops convert into lunchtime restaurants whilst maintaining the morning and afternoon style as usual. Many serve non-alcoholic drinks only, though most accept you with your own bottle of wine or beer, often charging a modest corkage, though not invariably. Several are licensed to serve wine, beer, or cider with food. All we can suggest is that you dive in as we did to the place in the book that you fancy. After a few visits you will find your favourites.

Essex is a wonderful county for walking and there is a huge diversity of interesting places here for you to enjoy. There are bright and breezy coastal walks, at Harwich and West Mersea for instance, and walks that take you into Constable Country at Dedham or the rolling hills and dales around Castle Hedingham. Wide views over the lovely countryside are to be expected, while castle ruins, ancient abbeys, great halls and restored windmills add to the interest. Some of the wonderfully attractive small towns of Essex such as Thaxted and Saffron Walden provide historic nooks and crannies to explore after your walk and cream tea.

Most of the walks, from $2^{1}/_{2}$ to 7 miles, are within the capabilities of the averagely fit person, certainly of walking age children, and almost all start and finish at or near the teashop. Occasionally the walk will start at a car park and visit the teashop part way round the route. In this case, if the going is muddy take care to remove offending footwear before entering. Otherwise you may not be too popular with the management!

So what do you need to take into account before launching out on a walk? Firstly the time of year. What protective clothing should you pack in the car? This could range through sunhats and overshirts to keep off the sun, waterproofs to keep off the rain and warm hats, jumpers, coats and gloves to keep out the cold. Do you think you will need to carry a drink? In fact we tend to carry a small bottle of water and stop on the route for a brief rest and a drink. We know of many walkers who far prefer to carry a small piece of fruit to eat at a similar rest break. On the Billericay walk the teashop is about half way round so this may save you carrying a drink or sandwiches on this the longest of the walks.

The sketch maps are only intended as a guide; we would recommend you carry the relevant O.S. map and, if you have one, a compass. It is so easy to lose your sense of direction on overcast days walking in a strange area. Your footwear should be suitable for the season. There are many times of the year when you will find walking sandals or trainers quite enough, but when the rains set in walking boots or even wellingtons come into their own. Also please phone the tea shop to reserve your table if we have advised in the text to do this. Many get very booked over the busy sessions and it would be a great disappointment to get there and find they are full. Park your car carefully to avoid any inconvenience to locals.

In the hope of meeting some of you on these walks, we wish you all happy times in Essex at the teashops and on the walks we describe.

Ann and Norman Skinner

Walk 1
WALTHAM ABBEY

This is a rather strenuous walk but the extra effort is well worthwhile. It starts near the ancient Abbey and goes over the Greenwich Meridian line, on its way to the Countryside Centre. You now enter the Lee Valley Park and walk along the delightful banks of Cornmill Stream through Cornmill Meadows. A short climb brings you to a height of 250 feet near Monkhams Hall where a conservation area with all-round views awaits. A descent brings you into Puck Lane, another climb and descent into Claygate Lane and, you have guessed it, another climb and descent on your way back into the park. Just under a mile's walk along the Greenwich Meridian Line and you are back at your car and the awaiting historic teashop, which dates back to the 15th century.

Philpotts Tea Rooms are situated in the old Lychgate in Church Street. Parts of the original one up, one down building of 1420 remain. Its downstairs beam and upstairs wall are intact. In 1540 at the dissolution of the monasteries, the property was given to the Lord of the Manor. He in turn 'obtained' part of the churchyard, so in 1610 the property was extended. In 1880 a bay window was added so William Winters, a local author, could display his books. The kitchen range dates from 1890 and comes from another local house. You sit amidst this history when you make your visit. We found tightly grouped tables with a blue and white theme. The china is all in blue and white with a wide variety of designs. The choice of teas included herbal, Earl Grey or lemon and ginger. Rombouts filter, or decaffeinated coffee, coke, mineral water, orange juice, chocolate, ice cold milk and milk shakes may also catch your eye. The range of cakes included carrot cake, scones with either cream or butter, jam tarts, mincemeat tarts, Waltham Forest Gateau, apple pie and ice cream and bread pudding. The light bites included soup of the day (delicious leek and potato the day we visited), jacket potatoes, sandwiches, eggs or beans on toast and main courses like sausage toad, sausage casserole, chicken and mushroom plait. You many opt for the Tea Set – sandwiches, scones, cream, jam, cakes and a pot of tea for an all inclusive price. Philpotts Tea Rooms are open daily from 9 am to 4 pm. Telephone: 01992 767641.

DISTANCE: 5 miles.

MAP: OS Explorer 174 Epping Forest and the Lee Valley.

STARTING POINT: The Information Centre pay car park, Lee Valley Park (GR 383008).

HOW TO GET THERE: Take the M25 to Waltham Abbey, exit then on the A121 – there are two exits and both take you from the junction to the car park. On balance we favour the old one that goes north-west under the M25 and is signed by a long series of brown and yellow signs all the way to the car park some 4 to 5 miles away.

ALTERNATIVE STARTING POINT: Park on the B194 about ½ mile north of the main car park. It's on the left-hand side of the road and called Cornmill Meadows Lee Valley Car Park (GR 384015). Join the walk by coming from the rear of the car park, signed Waltham Abbey. After about 50 yards head for the seat half-right then turn half-left; you have joined the Meridian Line at point 8 in the text. At the end of the walk at point 7 take the first left from the sign Waltham Abbey with the hedge on your left and follow this mown track with a small left and right squiggle back into the car park.

THE WALK

1. From the car park walk right (west) along the path, crossing the Greenwich Meridian Line on your way to the Lee Valley Park Information Centre. Keep an eye open for a small pavement slab which shows you when you are crossing the Meridian Line. After a visit make your way first right past the centre on a path that takes you north over a bridge and under the A121.

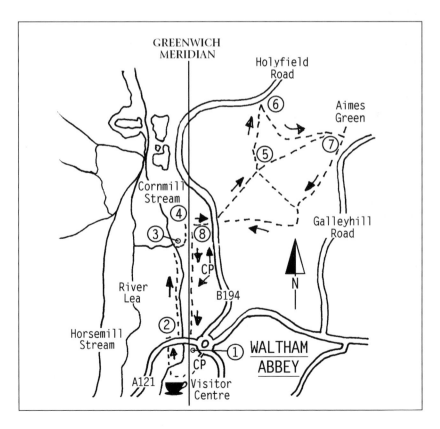

You may well stop to admire 'Nature Entwined' by Heather Burrell, one of the many works of art to be found in the park. The Lee Valley Regional Park is Britain's first regional park. Established by Parliament in 1967, the park stretches 23 miles along the River Lea from East London near the Thames at East India Dock Basin to Ware in Hertfordshire. The idea behind this 'Green Wedge' for London was to create a mosaic of land and water and mix together wildlife habitats, playing fields, open spaces and opportunities for a wide range of leisure activities. By 2000 many paths in the park had been developed for shared use and today provide walkers, cyclists, anglers, joggers, bird watchers, wheelchair users, parents with buggies, and doggy walkers with hours of safe enjoyment. The paths are well signed with the dual purpose blue and white parent and child sign with a bicycle underneath.

2. Take the second gate into Cornmill Meadows and walk ahead with the river on your right through two stiles until you come to a black metal bridge over Cornmill Stream. Turn right and cross the bridge.

You have been walking through a dragonfly sanctuary and may well have seen the Banded Brown Hawkers and Common Darters. Cornmill Meadows is a site of special scientific interest and is regarded as the best single site for dragonflies in Essex, Herts and Greater London; 20 species of damsel and dragonflies have been recorded here.

3. Now make your way left then right to walk with a high wire mesh fence on your left. Follow this round the corner until you come to a kissing gate with a sign to Fishers Green Lane. Do not go through the gate.

You have been walking near the old Royal Gunpowder Mills that date from 1665. They were closed in 1991 but may well soon reopen to visitors so watch developments.

4. Turn right and walk with a three-strand wooden fence on your left. Pass 'Travel and Discovery' by Paula Haughney and make your way out through another kissing gate at the far corner of the park

Nature Entwined – one of many works of art at Lee Valley Park.

with a sign to Galley Hill Wood and straight on to Aimes Green via Claygate Lane. Cross the busy B194 with care and ignore the no entry, private road signs. The next footpath sign is just past Eagle Lodge on your left. You go through a tunnel cut in a bush and climb uphill with a small wood on your right. Cross a gravel drive and go over a stream and up a flight of steps to join a well walked meadow path up the hill to the signpost and trig point.

5. Take the track half-left to a stile. You walk over another field to a stile in the same direction, then half-right to the corner of this meadow to find the stile in the corner near a stable. Walk down the green lane till the very attractive farm appears, then down the drive. Your right of way is just to the right of the gates.

6. Turn right at a bridleway sign a few feet further on and climb up

Homefield Wood, then walk down on Puck Lane all the way to the outskirts of Aimes Green, passing under some power lines.

7. Turn right when you reach the sign marked Galley Hill Green and walk past a countrified house on your right with chickens and geese that spill out across your path. Follow this lane up and then down hill for just over a mile till you reach the B194 again. The two signs for a public bridleway to Aimes Green and public footpath to Monkhams Pond can now be seen. You have returned to Eagle Lodge. Cross the B194 with care and return through the kissing gate you used on the way out. Those using the alternative car park return to their car park here, as described under Alternative Starting Point.

8. Otherwise return to 'Travel and Discovery'. Turn left on a mown path through the arboretum.

This stone carving was once a granite pillar on London Bridge. In 1964 it was removed and has been turned into this interesting monument. Its sister is about ³/₄ mile south of here and you will walk the Meridian Line as you wander south.

Pass a seat and cross a stream on your way. At the second monument turn right to cross Cornmill Stream and return to the cars the way you know. Follow your nose to Philpotts near the Abbey.

In Waltham Abbey you will find yourself in the middle of a town founded in the 12th century and many of its old buildings have survived. The market is still held on Tuesdays and Saturdays just outside the churchyard. The Abbey Church is well worth a visit. You will find King Harold buried in the Abbey gardens.

Walk 2
STANSTED MOUNTFITCHET

This day out is an interesting mix of old and new. You park at the edge of a Norman castle and village, and make your way along Lower Street out onto a link path to the nearby hamlet of Gall End. A series of field paths brings you to surprisingly delightful Ugley Green. This must be one of Essex's best kept secrets. Field paths lead you back, to pick up an ancient lane right back to Lower Street and an attractive teashop.

Michael and Natasha run the busy Mill House Tea Room in Lower Street, right in the centre of Stanstead Mountfichet. The wooden tables set in a pleasant tea room style are surrounded by a selection of antique bric-a-brac for sale, much of it displayed in a huge old fireplace. This is enhanced in summer by the use of the patio area and garden furniture so you can relax in the sun and watch the world go by as you sip your tea. You will find an array of speciality teas including Earl Grey, Lapsang Souchon, herbal and English Breakfast. A range of coffees, latte, espresso, cappuccino and decaffeinated, join chocolate, milk shakes, cans of cold drinks, orange and grape juice in ensuring the thirstiest of ramblers is well catered for. You can of course take your own bottle of wine or cans of beer and pay corkage to consume them with your meal. On the menu is the usual range of teashop goodies like home-made cakes, scones, puddings and crumbles. Sticky orange cake caught our eye. You are likely to find cooked breakfasts, hot sandwiches, home-made soup, and cream teas. The specials boards offered soup, fisherman's pie, steak and kidney pie, roasts, jacket potatoes, salads, ploughman's, omelettes, lasagne, scampi, and ham, egg and sausages the day we visited. The teashop is open 9 am to 3 pm Tuesday to Saturday and 10 am to 3 pm Sundays. If you can only do the walk on a Monday there are several pubs nearby. Ring 01279 816994 to book a place at the tea room or perhaps go back for one of their evening sessions run on Thursday, Friday and Saturday.

DISTANCE: 4 miles.

MAP: OS Explorer 195 Braintree and Saffron Walden.

STARTING POINT: There is a large pay and display car park right next to the castle and Norman village, just follow the brown visitor signs for Stanstead Mountfitchet Castle and Toy on the Hill Museum (GR 515249).

HOW TO GET THERE: The town is about 2 miles north-west of Stansted Airport. So head for junction 8 of the M11, take the A120 west to join the B1383 then north to Stansted Mountfitchet. All the time you will find brown visitor signs to guide you.

ALTERNATIVE STARTING POINT: As this is a busy visitor centre and the car park is huge I would advise walkers to just use the one start.

THE WALK

You cannot fail to notice you are parked beside Stansted Mountfichet Castle and Norman Village. This is the only Norman motte and bailey castle in the world that has been reconstructed on its original site. An early Iron Age fort, it was then a Saxon and Viking settlement before being conquered in 1066 by William the Conqueror. Until 1215 the castle remained a Norman stronghold, when it was razed to the ground in revenge against Richard de Mountfitchet II who then owned it and was one of the 25 Barons instrumental in forcing King John to seal the Magna Carta. From 1215 it lay forgotten and overgrown for over 750 years until its recreation. It is well worth a visit and any children with you will delight in the moving, speaking displays that greet you as you pass from hut to hut within the castle walls.

1. From the car park turn right into Lower Street, you may have time for a drink as you pass The Mill House. Turn right at the junction into Grove Hill (a cunning three-way set of traffic lights) and make your way up the hill till you come to Hawthorns and a concrete footpath

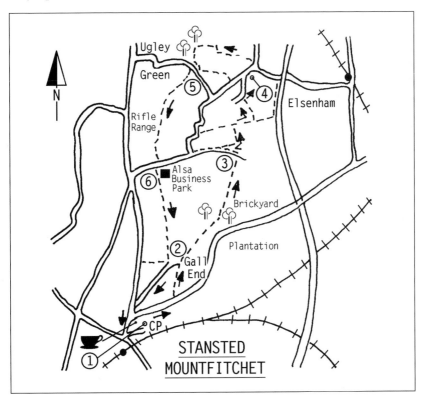

sign. Turn left and walk with a hedge on the right. Ignore the first two paths on your left. Then make your way downhill to pass Yew Tree Cottage at Gall End, a very small hamlet guarded by a network of paths.

2. Take the footpath marked 19 on the sign into a tunnel to the left of the garden, leading to a fence on the left. At the next direction post, head left diagonally across the field to the wood. Leaving Brickyard Plantation follow the waymarks across another field to join a grass track that brings you out to a narrow road.

3. Turn left along this tarred road, then right at the end of the hedge by the footpath sign. This rear of the garden path brings you round a field with Christmas trees on your left. Cross a stile and just before the second stile turn right. There is a yellow arrow to guide you. As you reach the next field you will find a yellow arrow. You turn left here and walk with the hedge on your left through the gates to a concrete footpath sign and the road. Turn right passing Lavender Cottage.

4. You soon come to the telephone box and bus stop – you have arrived at Ugley Green. Take time to explore and find the village pump and the old puddingstone nearby.

Some historians would have you believe Ugley should be pronounced 'Oakley' but the authors of Place-Names of Essex *are convinced there is no etymological justification for this and add the name really means Vega's clearing. Ugley and Ugley Green its near neighbour are rather straggling but very pretty villages. They certainly deserve to have better names, and what of the poor ladies of the local women's institute! Standing on Ugley Green you can turn 360 degrees and find in the centre of your line of vision a house, cottage or mansion each just a little more to your liking than the last one you saw.*

Make your way to the opposite edge of the green to the concrete footpath sign to the left of a hedge. Turn left and walk with the hedge on your right. You pass the most beautiful thatched house on your

Ugley Green is extremely pretty.

right. This grassy track becomes a field edge path as you pass the first of several yellow arrows. First the hedge is on your left, you then cross the field and a ditch is on your right. You now enter a small wood and immediately turn left. Half way down the wood the path pops you out into the same field you left but half way down. Turn right and walk out to the road.

5. Cross the road and walk down beside The Chase. Go through a gate where a yellow arrow confirms the route towards a kissing gate. Through this you turn right and left (on the maps we have the path used to go straight across) and you soon come to another yellow arrow and turn right through a hole in the hedge. You walk a well trodden cross-field path towards a big tree with a yellow arrow painted on it. Cross the bridleway and walk ahead with the hedge on your left. When you come to a gate turn right through the woods and left at the sign for a rifle range. Walk with the fence on your right all the way to the road where you will find a footpath sign and stile.

Ugley Green.

6. Turn right and walk down the road till you come to the Alsa Business Park, then left at the footpath sign. Walk with the hedge on your left. This well worn path follows the field edge through some trees and right down to the stream edge as it makes its way to North End House. Now take the white road ahead to pass the Dog and Duck on your way back to the route you know along Lower Street and your well-earned refreshments.

Walk 3
SAFFRON WALDEN

Saffron Walden is a very attractive old town, with plenty of nooks and crannies to visit after your walk. But first you head out into the countryside, where a series of field paths brings you up a hill to the side of Grimsditch Wood and wonderful views back towards the town and on to Little Walden, with the River Slade running through the valley. With luck you may spot fallow deer in the fields. A wide grass track leads on towards Butlers Farm and then a return route with superb views over the rolling countryside. When you get back to town, a teashop with a country feel awaits you.

It is surprising how so many businesses that look like teashops are these days named as 'coffee shops'. The Maze, at 9 Market Place,

Saffron Walden, is one such. The two largish rooms are joined by open stud work and the scrubbed wooden tables and chairs give a real old country feel. You will find the usual range of pots of tea for one or two plus speciality teas. Hot chocolate with cream or marshmallows, milk shakes, fizzy drinks, fruit juice and filter coffee are also available to quench your thirst. Chocolate fudge cake, banoffee cake, coffee and walnut cake, farmhouse fruit cake plus a daily selection of home-made cakes also await. For those who have worked up an appetite there are jacket potatoes, salads, and specials boards which include special offers on snacks like Bakewell slice and tea or coffee through low fat specials to quiches; home-made bacon and tomato was on offer the day we visited. Telephone: 01799 508117.

DISTANCE: 4³/₄ miles.

MAP: OS Pathfinders 1027 Duxford and Great Chesterford and 1050 Saffron Walden, or Explorer 195 for southern part of the walk only.

STARTING POINT: There is a free car park in Catons Lane next door to the football ground, also street parking nearby (GR 539389).

HOW TO GET THERE: Saffron Walden is in North Essex just south of junction 9 on the M11, on the B184 between Chesterford and Thaxted. When you arrive in Saffron Walden you will find a maze of one-way streets. Our best advice is to make your way to the north of town following signs to Castle Hill or Free Car Park or to the B1052 signed Little Walden. Catons Lane is on the west of the B1052 just as it leaves town.

ALTERNATIVE PARKING: There is a selection of pay car parks in the town plus some street parking near points 1 and 7 on the walk.

THE WALK

The name Saffron Walden comes from the flowering plant that was used for colouring and flavouring from medieval times and was commercially grown here, bringing great wealth to the town. Saffron Walden has been a residential centre for more than 1,000 years, with evidence of Iron Age and Roman occupation. The impressive church, mostly rebuilt in the 15th century, is nearly 200 feet long and its spire reaches almost that height, a testament to the town's prosperity. There are many fine buildings to be enjoyed as well, including the former Sun Inn in Castle Street with its impressive pargeting – this is said to be where Oliver Cromwell stayed with his general, Fairfax, during a dispute with the Army in the Civil War period. Just outside the town is the estate and house of Audley End, less than a mile from the start of the walk. Built originally as a house of Benedictine monks, at the Dissolution the abbey was granted to Sir Thomas Audley for services rendered and he built himself a house on a grand scale – it is open to the public. (Telephone: 01799 522399.) Saffron Walden School is also long on tradition. It is referred to in records dating back to 1317 and it was endowed in 1522 by Dame Jane Bradley, widow of a Lord Mayor of London, to support one teacher of grammar.

1. From Catons Lane car park walk north along the B1052. Between houses 48 and 50 turn right up Byrd's Farm Lane. This starts as a

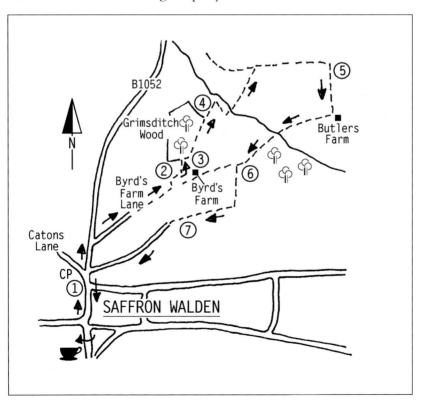

There are many fine sights to be enjoyed in Saffron Walden.

passageway or twitten. Cross the road into another twitten; this climbs and becomes a path between open fields. Ignore the bridleway on your right. In a few yards look for a yellow arrow on your left. Cross the concrete drive following the yellow arrows. Behind you is a lovely view of the town.

2. Take a turn right then go straight on uphill with a hedge on the right to the field end. Now follow two waymarks through the gap in the hedge and left to walk with the hedge on the left. You get good views left as you walk towards Grimsditch Woods.

3. At the 'Strictly Private Keep Out' sign turn right and walk right of the woods. You now get good views towards Byrd's Farm. Follow the edge of the wood as it turns left, passing another yellow waymark. Little Walden appears on the skyline and if you are lucky you may see the wild deer grazing below you. Tread softly or they depart at great speed.

Fallow deer have a pale appearance with reddish yellow speckles and were first introduced in England by the Normans. They are much larger than muntjac, the small deer from Asia sometimes seen when you are out walking. Fallow deer are now widespread throughout Essex, they love to roam the wide open fields where they mostly go unseen.

4. Your route ahead is with the hedge on your left to the next yellow arrow. Turn right beside the stream. When you see the old footpath sign to Little Walden go left over the bridge and walk the cross-field path uphill to yellow arrows heading slightly left. Turn slightly right and walk with a hedge on your left, and have good views all round from the grass track. Follow this track for about 1/2 mile till you come to a T-junction.

5. Turn right by the yellow arrow and oak tree onto a bridleway. Ignore the left turn by Butlers Farm but do turn right on the track a few yards further on. The footpath line is under the power cables and over an earth bridge. Now turn right by the bridleway sign, go under the power lines again and look for a single plank bridge near the corner of the field. This takes you to the other side of the hedge. Turn left; the route now runs up the field edge with the hedge on your left. At the woods ahead turn right and follow the arrows round the edge of the wood till you come to a track. Cross this and go straight on to a cross-path, you are heading just to the right of the distant church tower.

6. At a crossing track turn left (south) by the bridleway sign and walk uphill on the track. Follow this track out onto a plateau then turn right under a row of oak trees. The track becomes a red gravel path, before you reach a gate and some houses.

7. Your route back into town passes along Shed Lane and De Bohen Court. A twitten leads further down into Pound Walk. Turn left into Castle Hill and walk straight on at the roundabout into Common Hill. Turn right into Emson Close and left again into Town Hall Square. You will find the Maze Coffee House on your left. After your refreshments you may choose to explore this superb small town or just return the way you know back up Castle Hill to the car.

The Maze Coffee House may well have taken its name from the maze on the common. It is cut as a spiral in the turf. As long ago as 1699, 15 shillings was spent on repairing it. When you explore the town later you may well choose to include a visit to this maze. Saffron Walden's other maze, a Victorian hedge maze, was a copy of the one at Hampton Court and is of course in a corner of Bridge End Gardens. Visitors can still visit this maze nowadays but only by appointment: ring 01799 510444 for more information. The Gardens themselves are open to the public.

Walk 4
CHIPPING ONGAR

Chipping Ongar is an ancient market town with the remains of a Norman castle, and makes an excellent base for this easy stroll. The walk starts in the south of Ongar and crosses the Cripsey Brook – a substantial tributary of the River Roding. Two fine pedestrian bridges enable you to cross the Roding itself and reach the cafe via the castle mound of Norman days, with only a short walk from here back to the car.

 In the centre of the town is sited the Budworth Hall, built in 1886 as a fairly grand town hall. Part of this hall forms the Clockhouse Cafe. Here is served breakfast, lunch and afternoon tea, and throughout the period 10 am to 4 pm excellent tea or coffee is available. The cafe is open Monday to Friday (not Saturday or Sunday) for breakfast, a three course lunch and teas with cakes and other desirables! Telephone: 01277 362431. Nearby are two pubs, the Cock and the King's Inn, which will be open at the weekend.

DISTANCE: 3 miles

MAP: OS Explorer 183 Chelmsford and the Rodings.

STARTING POINT: The free car and lorry park in Chipping Ongar (GR 550026).

HOW TO GET THERE: From the A414 turn south at the Four Wantz roundabout through the middle of Ongar. At the bottom turn right past the Two Brewers public house and immediately turn right into the free car and lorry park.

THE WALK

The little town of Ongar was once a rural district in its own right. It was also formerly the final station of the Central line from London with a

A cross-field path leading to High Ongar.

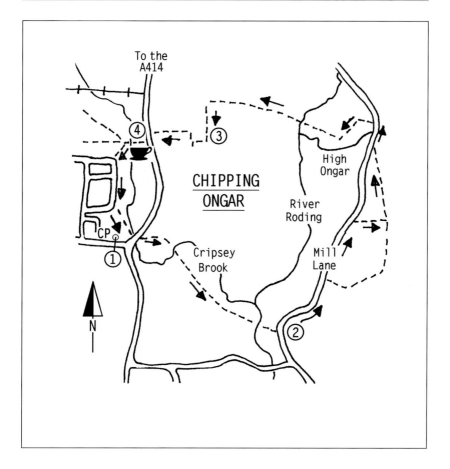

branch line from Epping. Nowadays Ongar is part of the Epping Forest District and the train line closed in the nineties. Possibly its most famous resident was David Livingstone, the 19th century missionary, who trained in Ongar in the nonconformist ministry prior to going to Africa.

1. Retrace your route back to the main street and cross the bridge over the brook. Cross the road and enter Bushy Lea passing some quaint old cottages. Pass through a kissing gate and bear right to a farm bridge over the brook. Turn left and follow the brook to and through a gap in the hedge. Now make for a metal bridge ahead.

Cows safely grazing by the footpath.

Cross the bridge over the River Roding and climb a metal stile to the road.

2. Turn left and follow the road uphill. Walk carefully as this is a busy road (Mill Lane). After barely ½ mile turn right on to a farm lane. After 250 yards look for a yellow waymark and turn left through a thicket to cross the field diagonally left downhill to a stile. Cross the road and follow the footpath to Millfield. Bear right with the hedge then turn right down steps with a railing. Follow this path to a bridge crossing the River Roding. Follow this path and join a field with the hedge on our left. Turn left at a playing field and at its end, right, carrying straight on to the castle mound at Ongar.

The Normans built a castle here in the 11th century, but only the mound remains today. The little town grew up around the castle and 'Chipping' is an old word meaning 'market', from the days when this was an important local meeting and trading centre.

3. Turn right into the car park by the Ongar library. The cafe is opposite

4. After your visit to the cafe turn left and left again (west) downhill over the bridge. Turn left for 170 yards into a housing estate. Look for a footpath turning left and leading to your car.

Walk 5
THAXTED

Thaxted's church spire and windmill beckon the traveller on from miles away, and they will not be disappointed when they reach this lovely old town, which was prosperous for many centuries first from the making of cutlery and then from the cloth trade. As this walk shows, Thaxted can also reveal many attractive little corners away from the main street. The route leaves the town via Walnut Tree Meadow and passes three old farms – Sorrell's, Golden's and Goddard's – before joining the infant River Chelmer. The return brings us back to the glorious church and something naughty but nice.

☕ At the Naughty but Nice Tea Room, the home-made chocolate and sponge cakes are where the 'naughty' bit comes from. Drinks are traditional and include Earl Grey teas, coffee and cappuccino, chocolate and soft drinks. In addition the tea room is licensed so you can have beer, lager and wine. Meals are available such as various home-made pies, cottage pie, steak and kidney pie, vegetables, soups, jacket potatoes, and sandwiches. Naughty but Nice is open 12 noon to 5 pm on Tuesday, Wednesday, Thursday, Saturday and Sunday in the months March to November. Telephone: 01371 831141. If your visit to Thaxted doesn't coincide with the teashop being open you will find the Star or Swan pubs able to welcome you with food and drink.

DISTANCE: 3 miles.
MAP: OS Explorer 195 Braintree and Saffron Walden.
STARTING POINT: Just past the church and the Swan Hotel turn right down Margaret Street to the free car park (GR 611312).
HOW TO GET THERE: Thaxted lies at the junction of the B184 and the B1051, about 6 miles north of Great Dunmow.

THE WALK

There are many features of this ancient town to be wondered at, none more so than the spire of the church which soars heavenward – a landmark for miles around. This church is the glory of Thaxted, of Essex, of Eastern England. It is a masterpiece of beauty, and makes Thaxted a place in which it is easy to understand how religion can enrich a person's life. Dominating the main street, which was and still is a market place, is the Guild Hall constructed shortly after 1400 for the Cutler's Guild with a double gabled roof on a building raised on stilts, making an impressive effect. Morris dancing was revived here nearly a hundred years ago and the town now hosts a gathering of rings from around Britain in late May. The road through the town divides at the Hall, where the left-hand fork leads to the windmill, and the right-hand twists uphill towards the church.

1. From the Thaxted car park turn left along Margaret Street and then right down Weaverhead Lane. At the bottom of the lane turn left along Copthall Lane. Soon as you pass the last house on the left, turn

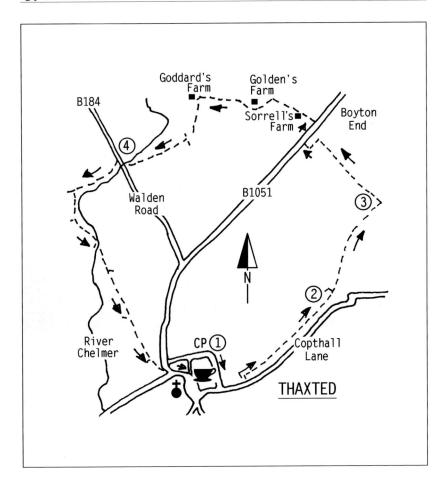

left into a path through Walnut Tree Meadow. Continue on your previous direction (north-east) with a hedge and a stream on your left.

2. At a gap in the trees turn left through them and cross a plank bridge. Do not turn on the first left arrow or to the right with the stream, but follow the edge of a small field to the left. Turn right and cross an earth bridge back on the other side of the ditch. Follow round the edge of this second field.

The 15th century Guildhall at Thaxted dominates the market place.

3. Just after a hedge turn left at yellow arrows, and walk with a fence on your left (including a kink to left then right) to the Sampford road. Turn right for 100 yards then cross the road into a wide farm track at Boyton End. Follow this past Sorrell's Farm, and Golden's Farm to Goddard's Farm. Take the track left out of Goddard's Farm and walk downhill to the Walden Road. Turn right and cross the River Chelmer with the road.

The Chelmer rises very near to the east of Debden and is but an infant when it passes Thaxted. It is one of the more important rivers of Essex and when joined by the Blackwater a few hundred yards from the sea it does seem unfair that it becomes only a tributary.

4. Turn left at a public footpath sign to walk on the right bank of the river. Turn left at Haslemere joining the Harcamlow Way and keep in a south-easterly direction.

The Harcamlow Way was created about 20 years ago by Fred Matthews. It connects Harlow and Cambridge in a massive figure of eight utilising many of the rights of way in the area.

Soon you join a back road which leads in ½ mile to the road junction at the church and the Swan Hotel. Just to the left is the top of Margaret Street, and you can walk down to your car. From here turn right back up a few yards of Margaret Street and cut through to reach Watling Street (the main street) near the Naughty But Nice Tea Room.

If you have extra time after your visit to the Tea Room there are some super places to visit. Thaxted Guild Hall is open weekends Easter to the end of September. Telephone: 01371 831339. Glendale Forge, in Monk Street, produces a comprehensive range of hand-wrought blacksmith-made ornamental ironwork with items for sale in the showroom. In the Train shed there is the Glendale Collection of unusual half-sized vehicles including Stephenson's Rocket. Admission free, open Monday to Friday 9 am to 5 pm, Sunday 10 am to noon. Telephone: 01371 830466.

Walk 6
BILLERICAY

*T*his walk is a fine mixture of town and country. You start out in open countryside, passing through the ancient dairy farm called Great Cowbridge Grange Farm on your way into bustling, historic Billericay where you will find the delightful Presence Coffee (and tea!) Shop. Now follows a fascinating stroll along the old High Street. Walk out of town via Tye Common Road and the new cricket stadium to rejoin the peace of the countryside and pass Blunts Wall and Bushwood Farms on your way to delightful Mountnessing Hall and church. The final descent takes you back to the outskirts of Billericay. This is a longer walk, with the teashop conveniently placed to refresh you along the way.

The well run Presence Coffee Shop is situated on the first floor above an interesting craft and gift shop at 48 High Street. The non-smoking environment is scented with freshly brewed coffee, and teas such as Assam, Darjeeling or the ever faithful English Breakfast. The wide range of drinks includes hot chocolate, milk, squash and orange juice. Talking of food, your energy levels can be restored with light bites like toasted tea cakes, or, if nearer midday, soup, jacket potatoes with lovely fillings like salmon and cucumber or chicken, salads, or sandwiches may entice. They do have a range of hot meals for those really starving plus the usual range of teashop cakes including chocolate fudge cake, scones, raspberry pavlova, brownies, flapjacks and lemon and honey roll. At busy times it is best to ring 01277 633009 to book your table. They are open from 9 am to 4.45 pm Monday to Saturday. Should you only be able to walk on a Sunday we would recommend the Red Lion public house as a suitable alternative.

DISTANCE: 7 miles.

MAP: OS Explorer 175 Southend-on-Sea and Basildon.

STARTING POINT: There is a large free car park at Hannikins Farm off Linda Gardens, off Mountnessing Road (GR 662958).

HOW TO GET THERE: Billericay is on the B1007 between the A12 and A129. Drive west passing the station, go straight on at Gooseberry Green roundabout. Between house numbers 330/332 turn right. Follow the sign to the recreation ground car park 50 yards away at the end of Linda Gardens.

ALTERNATIVE STARTING POINT: Park in Billericay High Street at the pay car park (point 2).

THE WALK

1. Walk back down Linda Gardens and right into Mountnessing Road. Take the first footpath on your left, marked 199 on the direction post. Turn left just before the second stile and walk with a hedge on your right to the next stile. Walk left and right round the garden, crossing the drive to cross a bridge and then continue ahead through a gate.

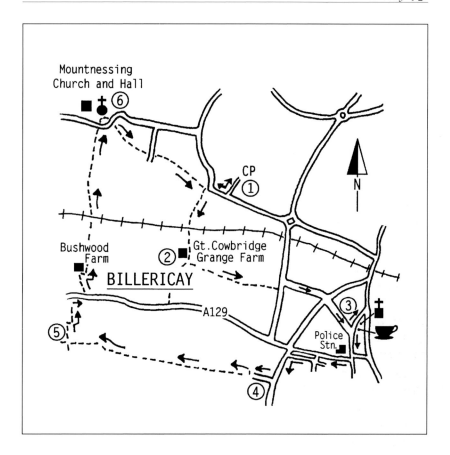

2. When Great Cowbridge Grange farmhouse is on your right take the stile ahead and immediately turn left and walk with a hedge on your right. You now walk in the same direction (slightly south of east) over a series of fields into Billericay, crossing a stile, two bridges and a stile near the houses. A twitten (passageway) leading left and right brings you out to the road. Turn left and cross the road to take the first road on the right, Station Road. At the next crossing road go straight across into Wakefield Avenue and Lion Lane. This brings you into Billericay High Street next to the Red Lion.

Your thoughts may well turn to Billericay's earlier inhabitants. Will it be Christopher and Marie Martin as they gather together with friends in 1620 to walk down Billericay hill on their way to join the Mayflower that is to take them as pilgrims to Massachusetts? It might be the leader of the Peasants' Revolt in 1381, Jack Straw, with his fellows just before they were caught and massacred in the woods nearby. Or is it Thomas Wood the Ghostly Miller who in 1763 succeeded in losing some eleven stones in weight by dieting on a mixture made from flour? The medieval brick tower attached to Billericay church has been ringing its bell over the comings and goings in the High Street for some 700 years.

☕ **3.** Turn left and cross the road at the pedestrian crossing to the church and then to Presence almost next door. After your refreshments leave the shop by turning left up the High Street, probably stopping to explore on the way. Just after the police station cross the road and walk parallel with London Road west on the wide grass verge. When you come to Gilmore Rise continue ahead to the junction with Tye Common Road, where you turn left and then take a right into Heath Close.

The Cater Museum at 74 High Street, Billericay is well worth a visit. Telephone 01277 622023 to find out more.

4. Walk down the road and straight on when you reach the field beyond. Walk west with a hedge on your left, cross the bridge and road. Walk straight on leftish to a kissing gate and now cross a car park to the footpath sign. Your route across the cricket pitch is between the playing areas to the footpath sign by the kissing gate straight ahead. Cross the track and go over the stile. Your route continues for about a mile in the same direction over two large fields on a well walked track to a bridge; you have been walking towards a pylon to the left of a wood. From the bridge cross to walk up the right-hand side of the field with some gardens on your right. Ignore the path off to your right but climb the slight hill. When the hedge runs out continue straight ahead till you come to a crossing footpath by a ditch.

The tranquil setting for Mountnessing Hall and church.

5. Now turn right and walk up and round the edge of the wood and out to the A129. Cross the road and then take the drive left up to Bushwood Farm, your way is well signed both with yellow arrows and direction posts. Walk right and left round the farm, picking up the path north-east to cross the railway line on the way to Mountnessing Hall and church.

Mountnessing is one of those strange villages that has its hall and church about a mile away from the main village which has grown up along the Roman road. The windmill adds to the countrified air of this busy High Street. The hall was built in the 17th century, and is still the centre of a working farm today. The church, built in the 15th century, is famous for its timber spire, which can be seen for at least a mile in any direction. An angel smiles across the nave of the church. The font is 15th century and two beautiful chests have 17th century carving.

6. After a visit to the church leave by the side gate and cross the road and then a stile heading south-east. The next large field has a well walked path leading over a series of bridges and stiles and across a road where you have to make a left and right movement to find the stiles. Now follows a series of smaller fields and a bridge across the stream. As you climb the last field edge with the hedge now on your left you will begin to recognise the houses. Cross the stile and make your way round the garden edge back to direction post 199, and take the route you know back to the car.

Walk 7
FINCHINGFIELD

This walk is a delightful mixture of wide country views, back paths and the beauty of a village some consider the best in Essex. The walk starts from the village car park along a path called Winsey Chase and soon you start to get views over the surrounding valleys and realise you are walking over a high plateau. Tom's Lane is the return route to Spinney Lodge and Spains Hall. Now follows a downhill road section back to Duck End and the excitement of the return to Finchingfield, its windmill, church, brook, village green, pond and nearby teashop.

Jemima's Tea Rooms are situated on the edge of the green and open for business at 10 am summer and winter. The dark wooden restaurant tables and chairs, patterned carpet, back room and garden service combine to endow the tea rooms with a welcoming atmosphere. You will find a wide range of teas (Darjeeling, Earl Grey and herbal), chocolate, milk, squash, and fizzy drinks. Bottled lagers, beers, ciders, spirits and wine are also available as an accompaniment to your meal. As well as crumpets, tea cakes, scones, and home-made cakes like victoria sponge, lemon cake, coffee and walnut, chocolate, cherry, carrot and fruit cakes, you will find a range of sandwiches, ploughman's, soups, jacket potatoes and blackboard specials like cream teas and lasagne. The day we went roast dinners were on offer and we had a delightful meal of roast pork, apple sauce and a lovely dish of freshly cooked vegetables. We resisted the temptations offered by the range of ice creams and special pancakes. Jemima's Tea Rooms are open 10 am to 5.30 pm Monday to Friday in summer, 10 am to 6 pm on Saturdays and Sundays. In winter the times become 10 am to 4 pm Monday to Friday and 10 am to 5 pm on Saturday and Sunday. To find out more and book your table ring 01371 810605. Alternatively, the Red Lion and the Fox public houses are nearby, subject to the normal licensing hours.

DISTANCE: 4¼ miles.

MAP: OS Explorer 195 Braintree and Saffron Walden.

STARTING POINT: There is a free car park near the village hall (GR 683326). Here you will also find some super toilets that won the loo of the year award in 1999!

HOW TO GET THERE: Finchingfield lies at the junction of the B1057 Dunmow – Steeple Bumpstead road and the B1053 Little Sampford – Wethersfield road. Coming north from Great Bardfield on the B1057 look for the car park signs as you enter the village and take the left turn opposite the post office, drive round the corner and up the hill till you reach the car park.

ALTERNATIVE PARKING: Park on the edge of Finchingfield village green or in the side road near the church.

THE WALK

Finchingfield is regarded by many as the most beautiful village in Essex. It is built round a big green that falls away to the pond by the brick bridge. The other half of the inverted pudding shape is filled by a windmill and a

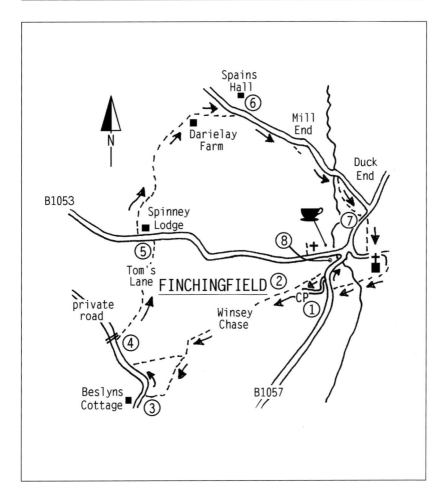

row of delightful old houses just oozing with charm. The whole is dominated by the church that has been extended and altered since the 13th century. On warm summer days a series of tourists just come to have a look.

1. From the main car park turn left onto a concrete path to the right of a garden hedge. Turn right and left with this to join the main public footpath that comes up from behind the houses on your right.

2. Turn left and walk with the fence on your right. You follow this path, Winsey Chase, for about a mile. It in turn becomes a wide green lane, does a left and right to walk beside a ditch, then becomes a wide lane between fields. Ignore the track on your right and descend to the footpath sign and road near Beslyns Cottage.

3. Turn right away from the farm buildings on a little used road. You now have a little climb to regain the height you only minutes ago so carelessly lost. It is a shame the hedge on your left is so high, it blocks the view towards Hawkspur Green and Little Sampford for much of the way.

4. Just as the road becomes a pebble track turn right at a public bridleway sign. It is narrow for a little while but opens up to become a track, Tom's Lane. As the track becomes a lane go straight on till you come to the B1053.

5. Take care here, the cars tend to rush along. You have to turn left, cross the road and make for Spinney Lodge on your right where you spot a public footpath sign. Walk just to the left of the Lodge. It can be muddy through here as you make your way through some trees to the footpath junction with a track from Little and Long Almond's Groves. Continue ahead to pass Darielay Farm (do not be tempted up the track on your left just before the farm building) on your way to the road opposite Spains Hall.

Spains Hall is the pride of the area set in 100 acres, with a lake made from two millponds. The house as you would expect is the best Tudor builders could design. Gables, porches, mullion windows sit alongside the work of art called rainwater pipes added in the 17th century. Much of the inside has panelling lining the walls and carefully carved overmantels.

6. Turn right and walk the road through Mill End to Duck End, about $1/2$ mile. Ignore the first footpath sign on your right and take the second black footpath sign beside a rather high stile. Walk over the meadow ahead. Your route is on a marked path to the right of the base of the distant windmill. Cross a stream and come out on the

Finchingfield church is fascinating and well worth a visit.

road in Duck End. Are the ducks you so often pass crossing this meadow descended from the forerunners that gave this area its name?

7. Turn left and cross the road and go up the steps on your right by the 30 mph sign. These lead you into a twitten, or passageway, that climbs steeply uphill and round several corners till you reach the road almost opposite the church. Cross the road with care and perhaps then spend a little time exploring the church area before you make your way through and out of the rear of the churchyard.

Finchingfield church has a massive tower first begun in Norman times and extended by a neat wooden lantern tower in the 18th century. The doorway, nearly 900 years old, leads to an impressive interior; you can see the Norman tower arch and on the south, 12th century arches. Additions from later centuries include carvings, font shields, an altar tomb and no less than a diagram of the old game of Nine Men's Morris.

Turn right down the lane beside the church and left at a footpath sign over the stream and out onto the B1057. Turn right and explore more of the village and its green before crossing it to make your eagerly awaited visit to Jemima's Tea Rooms.

8. Once you are suitably refreshed cross back over the green and look for the footpath sign beside a house called Moonraker. Walk right up this path to the point you recognise from the start of the walk, then make your own way back to the car.

Walk 8
CASTLE HEDINGHAM

Still, in the 21st century, like a piece of Norman England, the castle at Hedingham has an ancient stateliness unequalled in Essex and rarely bettered in the country. The composition of mighty keep and the church and village below makes every visit a thrilling pleasure. This walk starts through Falcon Square past the church and climbs north of the castle to Kirby Hall. Now it is downhill to follow the river Colne before climbing again to Little Lodge Farm and back to the centre of the village, and a memorable teashop.

A visit to the Magnolia Tea Rooms combined with a walk round the parish will make a day to remember. The tea rooms have always been owned by the Buckley family and are uniquely combined with a specialist cycle shop started by the son of the proprietor. Here you can have breakfast, lunch or tea. The menu is changed daily and of course features speciality teas, coffee, chocolate, and super home-made lemonade as well as sandwiches, tea cakes and cream teas. Open Tuesday to Sunday 9.30 am to 5 pm. Telephone: 01787 460197. Opposite the Magnolia Tea Rooms, the Bell public house offers refreshment daily 11.30 am to 3 pm, and 6.30 pm to 11 pm.

DISTANCE: 5 miles.
MAP: OS Explorer 195 Braintree and Saffron Walden.
STARTING POINT: There is street parking near the Magnolia Tea Rooms (GR 786355).
HOW TO GET THERE: Drive north of Braintree on the A1017. Through Sible Hedingham turn right on a road signposted to Castle Hedingham. After 3/4 mile park on the road.

THE WALK

1. Walk down past the tea rooms in St James Street to the Youth Hostel in Falcon Square. Walk along Crown Street passing the church on your left. Turn right and cross the road at Pye Corner and past Pye Cottage follow the concrete signpost up a track.

The church is almost as old as the castle and is an excellent example of late Norman style, well worth looking around. There is an impressive monument to a 16th century Earl of Oxford. There are also other historic buildings to enjoy in the village, including the old inn nearby.

2. Past the hedge turn left and walk uphill with the hedge on your left. As you climb look back to the castle behind you. At a junction of footpaths keep slightly left, walking north-west with a hedge on your right. Go under pylons and at the end of the hedge continue across an open field to the road. Turn right up to Kirby Hall.

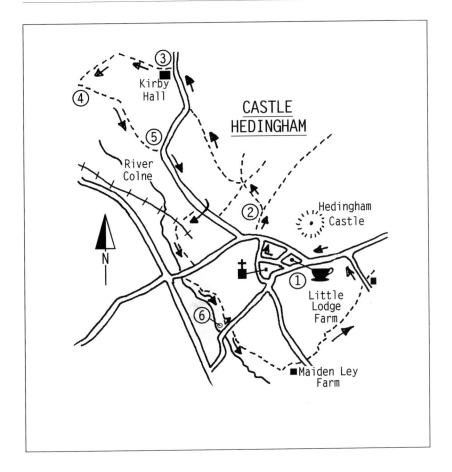

3. Follow the direction post to the left past farm buildings and take the track to the right and the left downhill to a yellow arrow.

4. Turn left across the field (south-east). Walk to the corner and follow to right and left with hedges on your left, to a road on the corner under a pylon.

5. Turn right for 600 yards past a footpath sign and turn right at a concrete sign walking between a wire fence and a hedge to cross the railway line. Turn left along a field edge and then right at the corner.

Cottages to be seen near Pye Corner.

When the houses end turn left to a road. Turn right along the road for a few yards over a bridge and turn left by a footpath sign to follow a well marked path through a nature reserve. The last 25 yards of this path were surprisingly overgrown with nettles when we were there last but we hope that this situation will have been cleared up.

6. Coming to a little road turn left and soon right at a footpath sign now with the River Colne on your right. Follow the path for about 500 yards to a T-junction. Here turn left past Maiden Ley Farm. Cross a road and walk up to Little Lodge Farm. Follow the path past a crossing hedge and turn left up the farm road to the main road. Now turn left back into Castle Hedingham.

Hedingham Castle itself is open from the week before Easter to the end of October 10 am to 5 pm daily. Admission charge. The splendid Norman keep was built in 1140 by the famous de Veres, Earls of Oxford, and the castle was visited by King Henry VIII and Queen Elizabeth I and besieged by King John. There is a banqueting hall with minstrels gallery and the finest Norman arch in England. Telephone: 01787 460261.

Strolling along the lane past Kirby Hall.

Walk 9
HALSTEAD

Halstead is an attractive little town in the Colne valley, but your route soon leaves the town behind to join a farm track with wonderful views out over the rolling countryside. You visit colourful Greenstead Green and its old church, and glimpse Stanstead Hall in the distance. Later you pass Greenstead Hall as you begin the descent back down into Halstead, where your progress to the riverbank teashop passes the fire station by way of an interesting series of town twittens or passageways.

🍵 Nestled on the bank of the River Colne right in the centre of Halstead you will find the Blacksmiths Riverview Restaurant and Tea

Rooms, once a blacksmith's forge. There are tables inside for about 40 people, plus the usual garden tables for those wishing to eat outside. The extensive menu includes all the usual naughties like fruit, carrot, and ginger cakes plus a wide selection of sponges, ploughman's, all day breakfasts, and a choice of main meals, Sunday roast and a tempting choice of desserts. The range of drinks includes tea, coffee, chocolate or squash plus beers, ciders and wine that are served with midday cooked meals. They have a daily lunchtime special for a very reasonable price, the day we visited it was cottage pie and a choice of sweets – the lemon meringue tart was lovely. If you intend visiting during the lunchtime ring 01787 478088 to book a table. It does get busy the later part of the week and at weekends. Opening hours are – 10 am to 4 pm Monday to Saturday and 11 am to 4 pm on Sundays.

DISTANCE: 4¹/₂ miles.

MAP: OS Explorer 195 Braintree and Saffron Walden.

STARTING POINT: There is ample street parking in Kings Road opposite The Electric Motor Co. Ltd. (GR 812303).

HOW TO GET THERE: Halstead lies on the A131 between Braintree and Sudbury. Coming from the south turn right into Kings Road at the first roundabout as you reach Halstead. There is a car park sign on the main road to assist you.

ALTERNATIVE PARKING: Park in Weavers Croft car park. Continue down Kings Road then turn right, follow the car park signs till you reach this large public car park. You can park here free of charge but there is a strict 3 hour time limit. You may have to move the car elsewhere at the end of the walk while you explore Halstead.

THE WALK

Halstead was built about a hill overlooking the River Colne. Many of its buildings date from the 15th century. It has long had links with the manufacture of silk and crepe. We first got to know it well about 25 years ago when it was still ruled by the weaving industry. We were fascinated to look out of our first floor sitting room window to watch the factory shift changes. About ten minutes before the Klaxon, drinkers would pour out of the pub opposite, and after the change the pub would again be full of eager

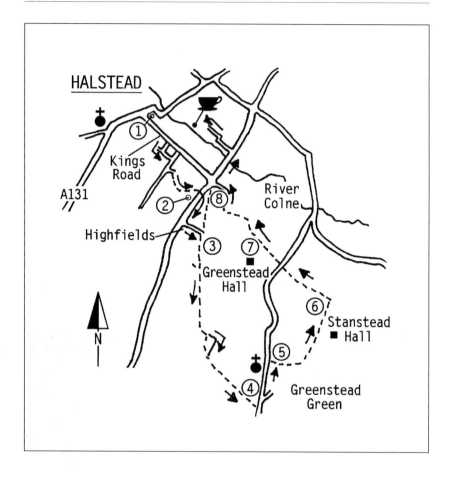

drinkers popping in for a quick half on their way home. We were delighted to be invited into a weaving shed on what is now Weavers Court to see what was going on. The noise was deafening as shuttles crashed back and forth on giant looms. The two most remarkable fabrics being woven at that time were parachute silk and elasticated panels for maternity wear.

1. From Kings Road turn right into Martins Road (uphill) and left into Neale Road. Now right into Mitchell Avenue. Cross Park Drive to a footpath sign. Follow the gravel drive past some garages on your left. Ignore the path off on your right and go straight on uphill. When the footpath becomes a gravel road turn right. You are now in School Chase.

2. At the road turn right, you have guessed it, uphill again, but the way is made more interesting as you pass the old Cooks Brewery and dream of long forgotten fermentations. A left turn into Highfields then immediately right into South Close brings you to a twitten, or passageway, between numbers 20 and 22. After about another 20 yards you have reached the fields.

3. Turn right south and walk a well-trodden path at the rear of houses on your right. It becomes rural and you go through a gap in the hedge to join a farm track that has come from the road on your right. Turn left along this still heading south. You now start to get wonderful views over the valley to Gladfen Hall and Plaistow Green. Follow this farm track for about a mile. During this time it turns right

The peaceful setting for St James the Great church, Greenstead Green.

and left round a couple of fields, at one point the footpath crosses a cultivated field but the locals all follow the track. All the time you will get glimpses of Greenstead Green church across the fields to your left.

4. When you reach the road you are in Greenstead Green. Turn left and then keep left at the fork. You are now passing the old houses as you make your way towards the church.

Greenstead Green is a wonderful mixture of old and new. As you get your first glimpse of the village you are surprised by a riot of colour pink, orange, green, blue and cream; you might even be in Ireland. Long gone are its windmill and two pubs. You will however walk past some old terraced houses, some well appointed bungalows and the Old School House that was built mainly of flint in 1844. Opposite is the church of St James the Great with its interesting spire.

A visit to St James the Great is well worth while and you may wish to sit in the sun as we did to have a bottle of water. After a rest make your way out of the churchyard and opposite the Old Vicarage turn right at the footpath sign.

Your route now becomes more rural with a cross-field route often taken by Rab Butler, the eminent Tory MP on his way to church where he sometimes read the lessons. You later pass by his former home of Stanstead Hall. He was once called 'the best Prime Minister we never had.'

5. This field path has a hedge on the right. At the end of the field turn left and again walk with the hedge on your right. The path here was diverted recently and you now walk with a fence on your right. When this runs out go slightly right and then immediately left to walk with a paddock fence on your right and later a hedge on your left. You can glimpse Stanstead Hall in the distance on your right.

6. At a gap with a waymark on your left go through and walk another field edge north-west and out to the road. Cross the road by Lodge Cottage and go up the drive for a few steps. You now cross a

The Old School House, Greenstead Green.

stile into a horse field. You are heading half-right to a second stile in the right-hand corner.

7. Cross the stile; you are now about level with Greenstead Hall but the building is mostly concealed in the trees. Your route ahead is well marked. You are heading for distant Halstead church and it is mostly downhill. At the end of the next hedge turn rightish and follow the yellow arrows across the field. More waymarks take you across a second field and out to a footpath sign, one meadow, and the road.

8. Walk straight ahead up Cooks Close. Take the footpath sign ahead between numbers 16 and 18 along another town path to a footpath sign by a house called Linden Lee. Turn right downhill (Balls Chase) and left to a road junction. Cross the road and walk in front of the fire station in Parsonage Street. Turn left up the footpath behind the swimming pool, passing the school, then make your way round into Weavers Court car park. Between Calendar and Solar turn left and left again passing Weavers to reach Blacksmiths Tea Rooms beside the river for a well earned rest and refreshments. Cross the River Colne on a footbridge passing Townsford Mill and make your way uphill back to the cars in Kings Road.

Townsford Mill is now an antiques centre, where you will find three floors of antiques and collectables displayed. This old mill was one of Courtauld's first silk weaving factories. Ring 01787 474451 for more information.

Walk 10
DANBURY

This walk is an interesting mixture, where even the car park has a view. A road walk brings you to the entrance to some lovely nature reserves, from where you make your way along the side of the golf course and into Thrift Wood. The route goes on past the Royal Oak pub, then on a track over open fields to Tyndales. Now follows another short road section till you reach the fields just before Gay Bowers Farm. You then follow a twisting path across Danbury Common, through the woods and pick up a public footpath system that enables you to climb to the church at Danbury. Having stopped to admire the considerable view you walk past the beacon before rejoining your car and making your way for tea. There is one point on the walk where you cross a stream, and boots would be needed in wet weather.

The popular Tea on the Green teashop is situated at the rear of the village pond at Eves Corner. It is open every day except bank holidays from at least 10 am to 4.30 pm. You will find a wide choice of teas from traditional breakfast and afternoon tea through Earl Grey, Lady Grey, Jasmine, Assam, Darjeeling, Ceylon, Lapsang Souchon and decaffeinated. Those who prefer coffee are not left out and can look forward to fresh ground, decaffeinated, cappuccino, Expresso Ristretto, Vienna, latte and mocha. There is a daily specials board and on the day we visited home-made soup, broccoli and cheddar quiche, salad and jacket potato followed by apple pie would have kept us going for 50 let alone 5 miles! You will also find on the menu a range of jacket potatoes, sandwiches which can be plain or toasted, various toasts and toasted breads and a fine selection of home-made cakes. You may be tempted by their full afternoon tea or the more traditional cream tea. Children are also well provided for with their own menus. Ring 01245 226616 to book your table if you are expecting to call at a busy time as this is a popular meeting place for locals.

DISTANCE: 5¹/₂ miles.

MAP: OS Explorer 183 Chelmsford and the Rodings.

STARTING POINT: Mayes Lane car park (GR 783051).

HOW TO GET THERE: From the A12T east of Chelmsford take the A414 (east) and climb Danbury hill. In the centre of the village just past the Co-Op at the roundabout turn right into Mayes Lane and right again into the car park.

ALTERNATIVE STARTING POINT: Start at point 2 in the walk at the junction of Little Baddow Road and Runsell Lane (GR 784057). There is a small but adequate car park.

THE WALK

Danbury is one of the higher villages of Essex reaching 107 metres in height near the church. In Plantagenet times Danbury was said to be most prosperous because of 'a plenty of fruits and the fertility of the fields'; in fact there was enough wealth for it to be divided into two parishes.

1. Climb the concrete slope out of the car park (north) and pass a

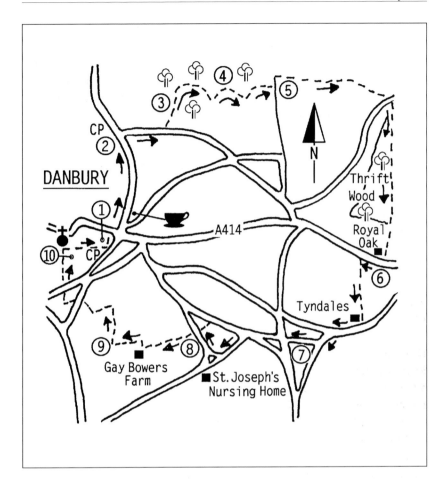

children's playground. Go through the gate and cross the A414 by Danbury Village Hall. Turn left into Little Baddow Road passing Bakers of Danbury and spotting the tea rooms. Continue along Little Baddow Road for about ½ mile walking past St John's School, and Hay Green.

2. Just opposite a car park turn right into Runsell Lane, then left into Clarks Farm Road. Pass a direction post leading to a public footpath. Just to the left of Litchborough Park join the footpath that takes you through a kissing gate into Spring Wood Essex Wildlife Trust nature reserve.

The Spring Wood, Poors Piece and Little Baddow Heath reserves through which you will be walking form part of the 250 acre Danbury Ridge nature reserve complex managed by Essex Wildlife Trust. Spring Wood is a 9 acre area of secondary woodland. Poors Piece sits at an angle to the west of Little Baddow Heath and is well known for its oak pollards. Litttle Baddow Heath is famed for its stream valley; plants like heath milkwort have been spotted on this reserve.

3. At the Anglian Water property do not go through the second gate but turn right on the forest track. Follow the main path on through a kissing gate and down a steep descent of about 20 paces (you are now in Poors Piece). This faint track joins with a more major facing track. Turn right and make your way downhill to some duck boards. Go over the stile and turn left.

4. Ignore the path on your left that recrosses the river and turn right uphill to the T-junction. Turn left, marked with an arrow. This brings you to a kissing gate and notice board that tells you you have now crossed Little Baddow Heath nature reserve. Turn left on a gravel road till you come to a house named 'Robins Wood'.

5. Turn right and after 12 paces pass a bridleway sign tucked in the holly bush. Follow along the edge of the golf course for about 3/4 mile till you come to a road and the entrance to the golf course. Cross the road to a gate and stile and footpath sign. Walk ahead to another gate, ignore the arrow to the left and follow the footpath straight ahead through the wood. There is no bridge at the stream so boots are needed in wet weather. Follow the main path on through the woods (south) to a gate and on across common land to the scaffold-pole stile and out to the road by the Royal Oak.

6. Turn right and walk up the A414 for 50 yards till you come to a black and white footpath sign on the left-hand side of the road. Cross carefully and make your way to the left of a metal farm gate then

Attractive cottages near the entrance to the golf course.

walk the track to Tyndales Manor and Farm. Turn right again, you are now on the B1418. Take the second turning on your right by 'South Riding'.

7. Now follows a road section. Go straight on at the next crossroads, signed Gay Bowers. Turn right into Capons Lane and left into Gay Bowers Road. Turn right at St Joseph's Nursing Home or take the unmade road right just before it, this is what the locals do and cut the corner. Walk up the road, passing the other end of the unmade road and look for a stile on your left.

8. Cross the stile and follow the faint path straight ahead towards the dip and up to Gay Bowers Farm. Just before the farm buildings take a stile marked by a yellow arrow right, then another left. Walk with a hedge on the left to a third stile hidden behind a stable block. Now go straight on through the kissing gate and walk down the hill to a further stile. Walk with the hedge on your left, but take action to divert at the very wet bit. When you reach the stile in the corner of the field cross it and go downhill to cross a boarded walk.

9. Turn right and follow the stream uphill; ignore the first left turn. When you come to some brickwork and waterpipes in the stream, turn left. Follow this path across a crossing track and continue in the same direction. Ahead you will see an open heath – Danbury Common. Head for the car parking area to your right and take a path just to the right of a distant red brick chimney. You are walking north. Go straight on at a crossing track. Ignore two paths on the right and with a blue arrow turn left to pass a park bench. Keep left past the post marked '2' and go out to the road (GR 781046). Cross the road just to the left of the Evangelical church. There was no footpath sign when we walked it out. Walk ahead till you come to a footpath junction, turn right as marked by the yellow arrow and walk uphill till you come out at the road opposite the Cricketers. Cross the road and climb up the steep hill ahead almost to the church.

Danbury church is well worth a visit; the pew ends house a remarkable collection of carvings. Against one wall you will find three crusaders carved in wood. In 1648 the sexton received sixpence for taking down the King's Arms from the church and in 1661 was paid twice as much for painting over the Commonwealth Arms. About 700 years ago, the Knights of St Clere were buried here, but the more recent story begins in 1779 when the lady of the manor, Mrs Frances Ffytche, died and they dug out her grave. The workmen found, about 30 inches below pavement level, a huge flat stone which covered a lead coffin – there was no name on the coffin. Further investigations revealed the remains of a young man well preserved in a curious liquid which half filled the coffin with many flowers and herbs. The villagers had seen one of the three Knights of St Clere. After the coffin was soldered up it was laid back to rest by the foundations of the Norman church into its original grave.

10. Just before the church turn right on a well walked path to walk past the beacon and downhill back to the car park and your well earned refreshments.

Walk 11
HADLEIGH

*T*his *is a good short walk for those with only a little time to spare for their outing. From the centre of Hadleigh make your way downhill with superb views over the Thames to Kent. You pass the ruins of Hadleigh Castle and may have time for a visit – the artist John Constable was here before you. Your descent continues to pick up a low level path that makes its way west between Hadleigh Marsh and Plumtree Hill, before you regain the height so recently lost as you climb on a footpath between Sandpit Hill and Adders Hill. The delight is you walk through a grassland area that might be anywhere in the Derbyshire Dales! You pass a reservoir before walking back to town and the teashop on a series of paths, roads, and twittens. There is also the opportunity to extend this walk by an additional mile in a loop around the castle ruins.*

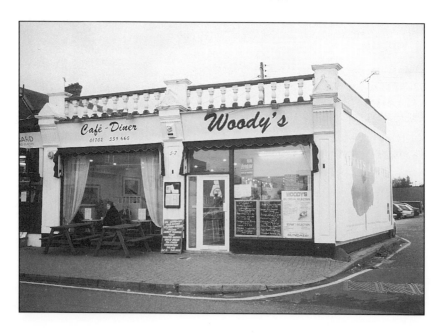

☕ You will pass Woody's cafe diner at the start of the walk as it is situated right next door to the Rectory Road car park. You will find it a well run modern establishment with polished wooden floors, wooden tables and metal and wood chairs. The overall colour scheme is a pleasing, light oak, pale green and orange. The choice of teas were breakfast or Earl Grey, lemon tea or herbal and it can be served in a mug, cup or by the pot. The range of coffees included decaffeinated, instant, cappuccino, espresso, filter or cafe latte. Hot chocolate and milkshakes together with a wide range of soft drinks like Tango, Pepsi, and cold milk should satisfy the thirst of the most eager of walkers. The range of food on offer includes the traditional teashop mainstay of cakes like carrot cake, banana cake, paradise tart, muffins and toasted tea cakes. However, those visiting at lunchtime will find a wide range of light snacks from soup to pizzas, garlic bread, all day breakfasts, sandwiches, baguettes, jackets, salads, a large blackboard menu and a range of children's foods. To round off your visit you may well choose an ice cream sundae or one of the wide range of Rossis ice creams. Woody's is at 5-7 Rectory Road, Hadleigh and the phone number is 01702 559660 if you want to check opening times. Booking here is not recommended as the establishment is not set up to reserve tables.

DISTANCE: 2½ or 3½ miles.
MAP: OS Explorer 175 Southend-on-Sea and Basildon.
STARTING POINT: The Rectory Road public pay and display car park, 60p for three hours, free on Sundays, which is plenty of time to do the walk and have a bite to eat (GR 811871).
HOW TO GET THERE: Hadleigh lies on the A13 between Benfleet and Leigh on Sea. Take the A13 east till you come to the church in the middle of a one-way system in the centre of Hadleigh. When you are level with the church signal left and go up Rectory Road for a few yards to enter the car park on your left.
ALTERNATIVE PARKING: Park in Castle Lane at point 1 (GR 809864).

THE WALK
1. From the car park turn right and walk past Woody's. Cross the road, using the traffic lights, to the church then over again with the

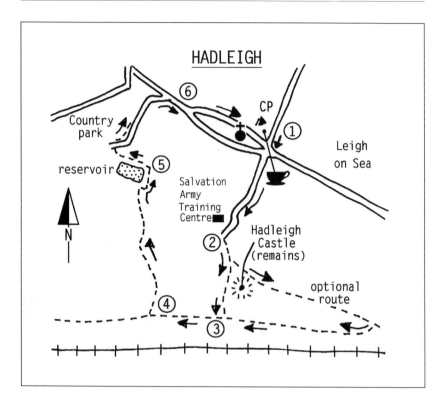

next set of lights to enter Castle Lane. Walk south through a small housing estate and pass the Salvation Army Training Centre. You then come to a very small free parking area. Go through the kissing gate.

The castle was built by Hubert de Burgh, and Edward I gave it to his queen. In 1365 it was rebuilt and made into a remarkable stronghold. The walls of the towers are nine feet thick. Henry VIII chose this residence for Anne of Cleves when she became his unwanted queen. John Constable visited the castle and painted the picturesque ruins in the early 19th century.

2. Turn left on a gravel lane. Ignore the stile on your left but go into the castle via an open gate in the railings. After your visit retrace your steps to the railings. [Those doing the extended walk should go back

Make time to visit Hadleigh Castle during your walk.

to the stile you ignored earlier and make your way downhill for about ¹/₂ mile, turn right and make your way back along the path that passes west below the castle.] Those doing the shorter walk turn left and cross the stile by the footpath sign. Make your way downhill admiring the views over the Thames to Kent. When you pick up a three-way footpath sign make your way right off the gravel path to a stile and turn right to go over it. [This is where the walkers who did the extended walk rejoin us.]

3. Walk on a path between two fields till a hedge appears on your right closely followed by a stile. Cross this stile on your right and walk with a hedge on the left till you come to the next three-way sign. You need the public footpath to Chapel Lane.

4. Turn right with a barbed wire fence on your right. Follow this over several stiles up the hill and through a valley and on up to a

The valley near point 4 on the walk.

strange concrete building. Walk to the right of this following the footpath signs then bear half-left to a stile in the corner of the field.

5. Cross the stile and turn left; you are walking two sides of a reservoir. At the next stile turn right and right again as indicated by the Public Footpath signs. You come to a narrow tarred lane and pass the entrance to Hadleigh Castle Country Park main car park. Keep straight on as a yellow arrow directs you up a field path to the left of the road. This brings you out at 66 Chapel Lane. Walk straight on up the road ahead till you come to Hadleigh Methodist church.

Hadleigh Castle Country Park stretches along the seawall from Leigh to Benfleet and took its name from 700 year old Hadleigh Castle. The park was officially opened by the chairman of the Countryside Commission, Sir Derek Barber, on 18th May 1987. It is a mixture of scrub, grassland and woodland and provides a place for plants and animals to live. You may find a kestrel overhead one day and flock of geese another, while those with keen ears will spot the 'call' of the green woodpecker. Its south facing slopes provide a good home for butterflies, whilst damselflies and dragonflies prefer the ditches and marshy ponds.

6. Turn right and go over the pedestrian crossing by the Waggon and Horses. Walk past Safeways and take the alleyway on the left between Pattens and Anglia. This brings you to the rear of the car park, a change of shoes and a visit to Woody's for tea.

Walk 12
COGGESHALL

A walk around Coggeshall and Coggeshall Hamlet is a walk through the pages of history. A stroll along the willow-lined bank of the River Blackwater begins this lovely route, followed by joining for a short time the long-distance Essex Way, running from Epping to Harwich. Here you pass the magnificent 12th century Grange Barn and the Abbey Chapel and Farm, before crossing a 700 year old bridge back towards the ancient streets of the town and a delightful 15th century teashop.

From amongst the teashops in Coggeshall we have chosen the Clockhouse. The little building which houses the teashop dates back to 1490 and the clocktower is Victorian. To spend an hour in the house can be a delightful experience, or in summer in the narrow rear garden can also be fun. As with many teashops these days, tea can mean Earl Grey, Assam, Darjeeling or camomile, and there is also coffee, chocolate, wine, lager and soft drinks. If you are hungry there are ploughman's, sandwiches, cream teas, high teas, and a selection of light lunch dishes. Telephone: 01376 563242. Opening times are Tuesday and Thursday to Saturday 10 am to 5 pm. Sunday 11 am to 5 pm. Closed Monday and Wednesday. When the cafe is closed, refreshments can be found next door at the Chapel Inn.

DISTANCE: 3½ miles.
MAP: OS Explorer 195 Braintree and Saffron Walden.
STARTING POINT: The Town car park (GR 848226).
HOW TO GET THERE: From the A12 drive through Kelvedon and near the river follow the signs to Coggeshall. In the centre of Coggeshall turn up Stoneham Street. After about 100 yards turn left, signposted car park, and soon come to the free car park.

THE WALK

1. Walk back towards the entrance of the car park. Immediately past an old red brick wall turn left along a narrow path. You pass some newly built houses. Cross a plank bridge over a stream (Robins Brook). Keep straight on past allotments and beyond a pond turn left at a waymark. Follow a path west through a field. Cross a farm track with a tall hedge on your right. Past an old factory building turn left to a road.

2. Cross the road and follow a concrete public footpath sign. Now take a track straight downhill past a football pitch and turn right to join the River Blackwater.

3. Follow the river upstream through the willow trees to an old pedestrian bridge. Cross the bridge and continue on the path to the

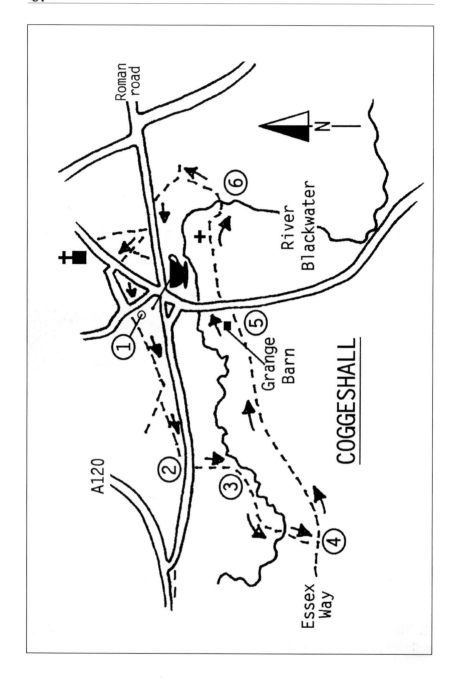

Roman road

N

River Blackwater

A120

Grange Barn

Essex Way

COGGESHALL

A bridge over the River Blackwater.

edge of the wood over another bridge and uphill to a farm track. You are now on the Essex Way.

This route crossing the county from Epping, 65 miles to Dedham, was opened in 1972. Some years later with the help of the Ramblers Association the route was improved and extended to Harwich – a total of 81 miles. In that period many thousands have probably walked all or part of the Essex Way and certainly the north and east of the county have been opened up to those of us who live nearer the centres of population.

4. Turn left with a hedge on your left and walk along the track for ³/₄ mile to pass the Grange Barn.

The Essex Way commemorative stone stands near the ancient Abbey Chapel.

It is certainly worth viewing the interior of the Barn. This magnificent 120 foot long timber-framed barn dating from the 12th century was constructed for the monks of the nearby Cistercian abbey. There is an admission charge. For opening times please telephone: 01376 562226.

5. Cross the road with care and follow a rough track downhill. Cross the bridge over the River Blackwater – it may be the oldest brick bridge in the county at over 700 years old.

In 1993, marking the 21st anniversary of the Essex Way, a commemorative stone was placed outside the Abbey Chapel at the halfway point along the 81 mile route. The chapel on the left is the only relic of the main Abbey building unfortunately destroyed in Tudor times. The Chapel was saved, as at the time of the dissolution of monasteries it was being used as a barn. Beyond is a group of buildings built at the same time, a house, a mill, and farm buildings of great antiquity.

6. Turn left along the path by the fence to reach the Roman road at Coggeshall. Turn left along the road and cross into the park by a footpath sign. Follow the left fork north-west and enter the brick-walled twitten, or passageway, to the road in the town. Cross the road and turn left into Queen Street. At its end turn right into Stoneham Street and make your way back to the car park. You will see the Clockhouse Teahouse at the south-east corner of the car park.

Coggeshall is undoubtedly one of the most interesting little towns in Essex and you will probably want to explore after your walk and tea. Once on the main road from Colchester to Braintree, it was bypassed some years ago, gaining more than losing in the process. You may like to visit the Coggeshall Heritage Centre in St Peter's Hall, Stoneham Street – a museum displaying items of local interest, supplemented by exhibitions on a theme relating to the past of this historic wool town. Admission free, open Easter to mid-October Sunday and Bank Holidays, 2.15pm to 4.45pm. Telephone: 01376 563003. There are many lovely old buildings in Coggeshall and certainly a visit would not be complete without seeing Paycocke's House in West Street. This delightful Tudor merchant's house dates from about 1500, with rich panelling and fine woodcarving. It is a National Trust property and there is an admission charge. Telephone: 01376 561305.

Walk 13
MALDON

The north west of Maldon on the hilltop is the oldest part of this historic town and this is a fascinating walk to the west and back by the river Chelmer, passing the old hospital, Maldon Hall, Beeleigh Abbey and Falls, then walking under the new northern bypass on the route of the disused railway line before crossing the Fulbridge and climbing up to tea.

 The traditional Saffron Tea Rooms offer a choice of different teas as well as coffee, cappuccino and wine, beer and soft drinks. Over the years the food menu has developed with breakfasts till 11.30 am, sandwiches, baked potatoes, starters and light lunches. Of course there is a choice of delicious cakes. The Saffron, in the High Street, opens 8.30 am to 5 pm Monday to Saturday and 10 am to 5.30 pm on Sunday, closing at 5 pm on Sunday in the winter. Telephone: 01621 856111.

DISTANCE: 3³/₄ miles.

MAP: OS Explorer 176 The Blackwater Estuary.

STARTING POINT: Park in Acacia Road opposite the Queen Victoria public house in Spital Road (GR 845066).

HOW TO GET THERE: Acacia Road is off the Spital Road at the Maldon end of the A414. Look for the Queen Victoria public house. The entrance to Acacia Road is opposite.

THE WALK

Maldon at the south of the Blackwater Estuary was once the most important town in Essex as all the produce went into and out of the county by boat from the Hythe. 'Don' means hill and the town stands on a hilltop above the water. London Road was once the route to London but after the new road was created passing Woodham Mortimer church, Spital Road was the more likely way. The north-west part of Maldon on the hilltop represents the site of the origins of the town.

1. Walk left (south-west) along Spital Road. Soon you will pass the remains of St Giles leper hospital built around 1164. Next you come to the site of West Station. This line was linked to South Woodham Ferrers and the main line to Shenfield and London.

2. Here cross the road with care and enter Maldon Hall Farm by a footpath sign. If you walk on the grass with a fence on your left you should turn left into a concrete track after 20 yards. Continue towards the buildings. What were farm buildings are now converted into rather grand domestic residences. Follow the path round to the right passing a magnificent barn conversion. The hall is over to your left and you go through a large five-barred gate. A long pebbly track goes to the north with fine views over the Chelmer valley. In 10 minutes you will come to a road. Cross this and walk downhill towards Beeleigh Abbey which may be visible through the hedgerow. This has been owned by the Foyle family and till recently an antiquarian book business was run from Beeleigh. The next important feature is the Beeleigh steam-driven mill. The walk continues to the Beeleigh Falls where the river Chelmer splits between canal and river.

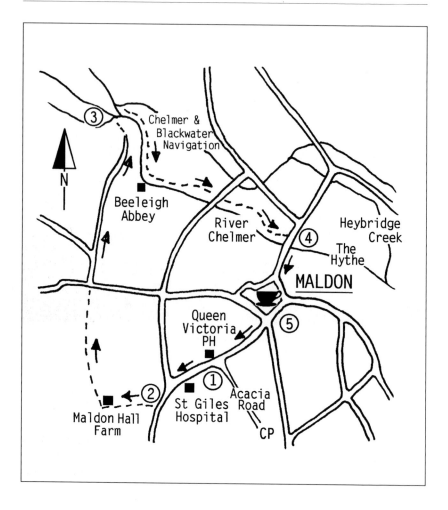

Close by the River Blackwater flirts with the Chelmer but is joined by the canal towards Heybridge. The Chelmer meanwhile makes a direct route to the Estuary only to be overtaken by the Blackwater 50 yards from the sea and renamed the River Blackwater. Such an important Essex river to be kidnapped in this fashion.

3. The walk crosses the falls and, just beyond a red brick bridge, turns right into a little path among bushes, which follows the left

The river and the canal part company at Beeleigh Weir Falls.

bank of the Chelmer. Ahead you will see the Tesco Stores constructed to resemble a railway station. Pass the Post Office depot.

4. Come out to the Causeway. Turn right over Fulbridge and up Cromwell Hill. At the top turn left past the Blue Boar Inn and right through to the High Street. A few steps further bring you to the Saffron Tea Rooms.

5. After leaving the Saffron walk along Spital Street. You come to the Ware pond, once the centre of village life for washing. Next pass St Peter's Hospital, formerly the Union House. It was built in 1873 to accommodate the poor. From here it is but a few yards back to Acacia Road.

After your refreshment it is worth the effort to view Maldon's millennium tapestry (in 1999 not 2000) at the Maeldune Centre, Plume Building,

A sailing barge returns to the Hythe.

Market Hill/High Street. The 42 foot long Maldon embroidery celebrated the 1,000th anniversary of the Battle of Maldon. The new heritage centre also displays items of local history and paintings. Open seven days a week April to September 10.30 am to 4.15 pm. Maldon District Museum, 47 Mill Road, is a traditional museum exhibiting a changing selection of objects associated with the area and the people of Maldon District. Promenade Park recreation ground is adjacent.

Walk 14
TIPTREE

*O*nce the great forests of Essex covered this area, now fruit trees stand in ordered rows and are a colourful sight in blossom. This is a very suitable walk for this book as this is where Wilkin & Sons' Tiptree jams come from, which must have been an ingredient in many a memorable tea! The route soon leaves the outskirts of Tiptree to walk by the Wilkin's orchards. Then from the ridge by the water tower you have views across part of the Blackwater estuary. Soon you come to the old railway line from Kelvedon to Tollesbury, which alas is no longer, and a well marked path through the fields brings you past the factory gatehouse back to your car.

☕ In the last years of the 20th century Wilkins opened a teashop for casual visitors. Having browsed through the books and preserves which are on sale, the following teas are on offer: Assam, Ceylon, Darjeeling and Earl Grey. Also coffee, a wide selection of sandwiches, plain or toasted, soup of the day, or ploughman's. We suggest that you walk before your visit to the teashop as you cannot conveniently do the walk directly from there. Opening times are Monday to Saturday 10 am to 5 pm. Sunday (July and August only) 10 am to 5 pm.

DISTANCE: 4¼ miles.
MAP: OS Explorer 183 Chelmsford and the Rodings and 184 Colchester.
STARTING POINT: The public footpath from Station Road (GR 897158).
HOW TO GET THERE: From either Maldon or Colchester travel on the B1022. At the southern end of Tiptree turn east along Station Road. After 700 yards stop at a public footpath sign on the right and park where convenient.

THE WALK
1. Walk south into Cherry Chase for 50 yards and turn right at a large Private Road sign. Turn right, eventually passing between fencing and hedges at the back of houses

Legend has it that smugglers brought their contraband from the creeks up the long hillside road, and hid them in the windmill. The Wilkin family have run the famous jam and marmalade factory for generations. The firm distinguishes between its various products with the delicacy of a wine merchant assessing his ports and clarets.

2. Turn left on reaching a narrow road. Follow a hedge on your left through the orchard. At the end of the orchard turn left over a stile and soon reach a bridge. Turn right and left along the field edge, following round to the right and left over another bridge. Follow this path through the woods and reach Tudwick Road.

3. Turn left along the road. When the road turns left go straight on at a public bridleway sign. When you come to a large water tower turn

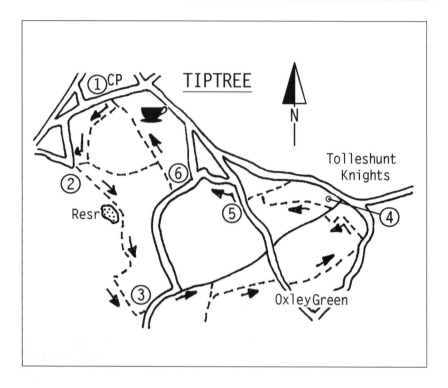

right across the field to a waymark arrow by some tall trees. Now turn left (east) and follow the path with a tall hedge soon joining you on your left. There are fine views of the Blackwater estuary to your right before you reach Oxley Green.

The estuary is reputedly one of the finest semi-enclosed areas of sea water on the east coast of England, listing amongst its famous historic points, Roman invasion, Danish occupation, the world's best oysters, and life as a strategic naval area in World War I. Among the islands in the estuary is Osea which can only be reached by boat, or by motor at low tide across the Roman causeway. Yes, the Blackwater is an exciting backdrop for the present day pleasure sailor.

Turn right for a few yards along the road, then cross the road and walk along a rough grass track over the field. Just before reaching a

Trees tower over one of the authors on a field edge footpath.

railway bridge turn left over a stile. Cross two more stiles into the playing field at Tolleshunt Knights. Make for the village hall and on to the road. Turn right for a few yards.

4. Turn left over a stile and follow the path parallel to the right-hand hedge. Soon turn left to the road over a stile.

5. Turn right past the Rose and Crown, cross the road into Strawberry Lane. At the end of the lane turn left along Tudwick Road.

6. Turn right at a public footpath sign and follow the well marked path back towards the jam factory. Continue past a pink gatehouse to Station Road and your car.

Now drive east to a T-junction. Turn right for a few yards and right again into the Wilkins teashop car park. (For safety reasons you are advised not to take a direct pedestrian route from the pink house to the teashop as this area contains large farm machinery and is in any case not a right of way.)

Walk 15
BURNHAM ON CROUCH

*B*urnham on Crouch is an ideal starting point for this walk with a maritime flavour. From the country park, you cross the railway to Ostend where you are rewarded with river views of this famous nautical centre. Soon your reach Creeksea, a tiny traditional sailing centre, then it is along to and around the bustling marina back to your car and an outstanding teashop. Burnham is popular with sailors and there is always something to watch on the water, as well as having many attractive buildings to enjoy around the quayside.

Howard and Moira Watling preside over the Copper Kettle, we think one of the best teashops in Essex. It is open 10 am to 5.30 pm Monday to Friday and 10 am to 6 pm Saturday, Sunday and Bank Holidays. During winter months the shop is closed on Wednesday. There is a large range of teas including regular, Darjeeling, mint, lemon, Earl Grey, decaffeinated, Lapsang Souchon, Green Gunpowder, and Mango Indian. There is also filtered coffee, cappuccino, chocolate, milk, milk shakes and soft drinks. Food includes breakfasts all day, jacket potatoes with all the fillings, home-made soup, chilli con carne, chicken korma and steak and kidney pie. A two course roast lunch is on offer but this should be ordered in advance of your visit. The owners have been at the Copper Kettle for many years and are justifiably proud of the number of regular customers who visit them. The Copper Kettle is in the High Street. Drive back towards the library and turn right downhill for 50 yards. The teashop is on your right. Telephone: 01621 782203. When the teashop is closed, the town boasts a range of excellent restaurants offering superb food from local fish to exotic dishes.

DISTANCE: 4 miles.
MAP: OS Explorer 176 Blackwater Estuary.
STARTING POINT: Riverside Park car park (GR 945957).
HOW TO GET THERE: From the A414 at Woodham Mortimer join the B1010 or from Maldon join the B1010 via the B1018. The B1010 runs into Burnham. Pass the station into the town centre. After Hillside Road on the right just past the library turn right at a sign to Riverside Park. Pass the Sports Centre on your right and turn left into a track at a parking sign, 50 yards later park in a section near the sea wall.
ALTERNATIVE PARKING: Just beside the library there is parking for about 15 cars. If you park there the journey to the main park will be on foot.

THE WALK

Burnham originally grew up around the parish church of St Mary, but during the Middle Ages the centre of the town moved to the quayside, taking advantage of the growth in seaborne trade. Sailing is a popular pastime throughout the year. In fact, the country park was created in part from the excavation hole dug out to build the yacht marina not long ago. Burnham

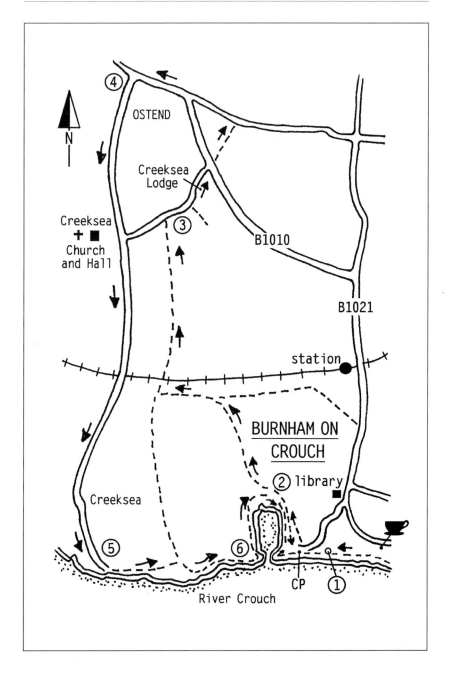

OSTEND

N

Creeksea
Lodge

Creeksea
✝ ■
Church
and Hall

③

B1010

B1021

station ●

BURNHAM ON
CROUCH

② library ■

Creeksea

⑤

⑥

CP ①

River Crouch

④

Attractive properties along the waterfront.

Week in August attracts eminent sailors from all over the country, when the Royal Corinthian Yacht Club has many famous moments to recall. Many of the substantial town houses which front the river and quayside are listed buildings.

1. From the Riverside Park car park walk up towards the sea wall. Just before reaching the wall turn right in the park. Walk north past the Yacht Harbour.

2. Just north of the car park, cross the access road and join a path leading to the public footpath running west, parallel to the railway line. After 500 yards turn right through white kissing gates and cross the tracks. The path goes straight on between crops and joins a path with a hedge on your left.

3. Turn right when you reach a road. Pass Fairway Cottage, and later Creeksea Lodge with a large pond. Cross the B1010 and enter a public footpath. At the end of the fence bear left through rough grassland. At a road turn left and join the B1010 at Ostend.

4. After 20 yards turn left across the road and follow the road to Creeksea. In the distance you will glimpse the church tower of Canewdon. Pass Creeksea Hall and the parish church. Beyond the golf course the road goes under the railway line. Next to a fine thatched house called Keeway, walk round a bend to the delightful sight of the river ahead.

Creeksea is a very old settlement, with Roman stone and brick work still to be found in its church. Creeksea Hall was originally built in the 13th century. It must have been a lonely place in the past, ideal for the smugglers who operated in the area!

5. Now walk along the river front, soon coming to the Marina which impedes your easterly progress.

Burnham Marina bristles with masts.

6. Turn left and round the harbour edge, in due course returning to the riverside. Almost immediately a metalled path bears left and takes you downhill to your car.

After your visit to the Copper Kettle you may want to find out more about this attractive town. The Burnham Museum is housed in a renovated boat shed on the quay, between the Burnham Sailing Club and Crouch Yacht Club. It contains many exhibits of maritime and agricultural interest. Telephone: 01621 783444/782562.

Walk 16
WEST MERSEA

Walking on a small island is always an enjoyable activity. Mersea Island lies tucked between the estuaries of the Colne and the Blackwater and from West Mersea the walk progresses from a charming village to the coast and back. You enjoy views of the surrounding water and the many craft afloat, traversing to the top of the island, which has been settled since Roman times, and making your way back on the north sea wall, finishing the walk by the ancient church and a welcoming teashop.

The Curiosi-Teashop is conveniently placed by the entrance to the library car park in a modern building opposite the library. Here you may enjoy a selection of traditional teas, Earl Grey, coffee, cappuccino, chocolate and soft drinks, as well as delicious home-made cakes. At most times of the day very reasonably priced sandwiches, rolls, baked potatoes, and soup are available, with such fillings as cheese, tuna, chilli and egg, prawn and lobster mayonnaise. Each table is named after a local place, Pyfleet, Strood, Colne etc. Opening times are Monday to Saturday 10 am to 4.30 pm. When the teashop is closed, the nearby White Hart public house is open daily from 12 noon to 10.30 pm.

DISTANCE: 4 miles.
MAP: OS Explorer 184 Colchester, Harwich and Clacton on Sea.
STARTING POINT: Library car park, West Mersea (GR 009125).
HOW TO GET THERE: Approach by the B1026 from Maldon or the B1025 from Colchester. The B1025 crosses the Strood into Mersea and the right fork leads into West Mersea. Just before the church on the right is the library and a free car park. As you enter the car park the teashop is on the right.

THE WALK

1. Leaving the car park pass the library and the teashop and turn right down the High Street. Opposite the church pass the White Hart and immediately turn right into Church Road past a succession of shops on either side giving on to residential houses. At the end of this road after 100 yards follow a concrete public footpath sign into a narrow twitten or passageway. This turns right and then left, then crosses a road (St Peter's Road) into a continuation twitten to another road. Cross this into Rosebank Road and then cross the next road into Firs Chase.

2. At The Lane turn right following a concrete public footpath sign and walk eastward, soon passing behind a caravan site to a view of the north-west coast of the island. The path follows directly along the edge of a field on to a gravel track out to a road at the entrance to a bowling green.

3. A few yards further on turn left at a footpath sign onto a path

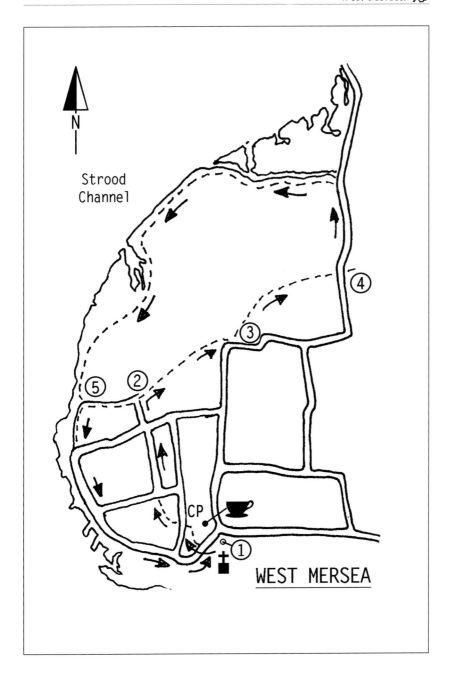

The Saxon West Mersea church with its massive square tower.

between two wire fences out to a field. Walk diagonally right to a field corner, turn right along the headland and then continue straight on to a pretty timbered cottage by the main road (B1025).

4. Here turn left and walk downhill with care for 300 yards to a footpath sign. Turn left along the sea wall. This path leads to the side of the Strood and you follow this walking south-west for over a mile to the outskirts of West Mersea. Enjoy the brilliant open views and huge skies.

Mersea Island is sited off the mouth of the River Colne and must have been of great significance to the Romans, at the junction of the Blackwater and the Colne. Other remains found on the island were of Saxon and Danish origin. Over the top of the island, separating it from the mainland, flows the Pyfleet Channel, where the best of all oysters are encouraged to put on weight. The main village is West Mersea and certainly this is the main centre of population.

5. On reaching the lifeboat station turn left and right along the front, past the slipway and walk past oyster pits to reach the island's church. It is a short step from here to the library car park and the welcoming Curiosi-Teashop.

The church dates from Saxon times and the tower is a massive 12 feet square. We must believe that this mouth of the Blackwater river was a Roman centre of importance. Mersea Island Museum in the High Street has much of local interest, including local history, natural history and social history, marine tools, wildlife, fossils, fishing and a fisherman's cottage of the 1920s. Admission charge. Open May to September, Wednesday to Sunday 2pm to 5pm. Telephone: 01206 385191.

Walk 17
DEDHAM

A walk from the heart of beautiful Dedham with its links with Constable, Gainsborough and Munnings. You make your way along the brook and towards the mill before leaving the village to walk along Donkey Lane and climb the track darkly named Dead Lane, enjoying superb views over the Stour valley as you head for a short visit to East Bergholt. Another high level path takes you to Gosnalls Farm and eventually down to Flatford Mill. The return route is along the banks of the River Stour passing Fen Bridge and Dedham Hall, perhaps for a cream tea in a 16th century teashop.

Dedham

The Essex Rose Tea House, a superb 16th century tea room-cum-shop, is situated in the centre of the village just across the road from the church. You will find the usual teashop goodies such as a selection of Ceylon, Earl Grey, Darjeeling and house blend teas, coffee, wine and fruit juice. This, with the choice of eclairs, wicked muffins, scones, biscuits and gateaux will surely more than satisfy most teashop walkers. On top of this you will find a wide choice of starters, salads, sandwiches and cream teas. The special offers board featured gateaux and a pot of tea the day we visited, just what was needed to restore the energy levels after a leisurely walk. Ring 01206 323101 to make a booking or find out more about the tea house. Open daily 9.30 am to 5.45 pm. Alternatively, Dedham has several other teashops, two pubs and a restaurant.

DISTANCE: 4½ miles.
MAP: OS Explorer 196 Sudbury, Hadleigh and Dedham Vale.
STARTING POINT: Public car park in Dedham village centre (GR 058334).
HOW TO GET THERE: Dedham lies on the Essex-Suffolk border north-east of Colchester. From the A12T ½ mile north of the Langham turn off, take the signed route to Dedham. Turn left past the church into the car park.
ALTERNATIVE STARTING POINT: There is a public car park in East Bergholt (GR 069347) near point 5 on the walk route. Walk up to the church then follow the walk directions from there.

THE WALK

Dedham was an important centre for the wool industry. Both weaving and merchanting were done from here. Dedham church was built about 1500. Thomas Webbe was one of its earliest benefactors. He was one of the town's princely merchants and reputed to have had Dedham church built in 1500. His body is buried in the north aisle under a richly carved tomb. He built his battlement tower so that a carriage could pass beneath it. Sir Alfred Munnings lived and worked at Castle House, Dedham, for 40 years, and a large collection of his paintings is on show there at the art museum. Telephone 01206 322127 for opening hours.

1. From the rear of the car park cross the stream and turn left and

105

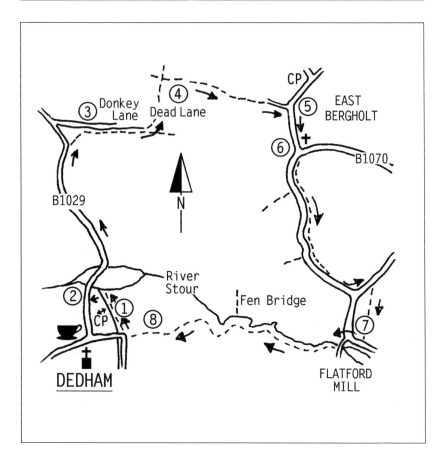

walk with the stream on your left. At a track turn left and cross the river and walk out to the road.

2. Turn right and walk past the mill, the Mill Stream restaurant, boats for hire and the Riverside Tea Rooms. Follow the road northish for just under ½ mile. As the road takes a sharp bend left, you walk right following the direction of the signpost to cross a field on a well walked path.

3. By a white house turn right along a gravel path. This is called

Donkey Lane. It soon becomes a wider green lane. At the wooden footpath sign marked 'E. Bergholt' turn left. Follow this uphill; you are now on Dead Lane. When you come to a wooden sign marking the junction of two footpaths turn right.

4. Walk the field edge with a fence on you left. You have superb views down across the valley from here. The path goes on through a gap in the hedge then slightly right to walk to the left of a house in the valley bottom. Cross a bridge and climb the hill ahead. The path becomes a metalled road as it leads you past Constable's early studio into the centre of East Bergholt.

You pass the site of Constable's childhood home on the way. Just to the left of the main church building, you will find the bell cage where the bells were rung for nearly 300 years till a prohibition order was served in January 2000 on safety grounds. You may wish to spend a while here exploring the unspoilt village before you regain the route.

5. Turn right and walk towards the church. Leave the churchyard from the small gate in the south wall.

6. Cross the road with care passing the memorial and taking the road ahead. You very soon find a narrow path on your left that follows the line of the road for about ½ mile. When it runs out you are in the valley bottom near the main Flatford car park. Take the road uphill with care, it is very busy on warm summer weekends. Ignore the entrance to the car park and the next road on your right. Walk past Hay Barn and one field uphill on the right your route turns sharp right and crosses a stile. This cross-field path allows you to stop and admire the rear of beautiful Hay Barn. You cross a stile and later change sides of the hedge as you descend to Flatford Mill.

Flatford Mill is perhaps known to everyone because of the paintings of John Constable; in fact the area is called Constable Country by the tourist industry. Many visitors just come to see what so inspired the great master. Today at Flatford Mill you will find a busy tea room, gift shop and small museum. There is a painting school just up the road and on a warm

Flatford Mill tea rooms nestle beside the river.

afternoon it is common to find groups out trying to follow in Constable's footsteps.

7. Turn right for the tea rooms, the toilets are right again. You may well wish to stop here for a mid-walk rest and a drink, or to explore. Leave Flatford Mill area by crossing the river bridge and taking the first footpath on the right (west). You have a chance to work the 'push handle and lift bar' cattle gate. It is great fun if there are four or five of you to all squeeze through together. Now follows a very pleasant riverside stroll. You basically take the route you choose, either close to the bank or further to the left. Either way you pass Fen Bridge and come to a kissing gate, bridge and kissing gate. From here your well walked route takes you leftish across a meadow to a gate and on between the fences. Ignore the path that joins from you

Bridge Cottage, Flatford.

left. You are heading towards Dedham church which now dominates the sky ahead.

8. A gravel track takes you to the left of the farm and out to the road. Immediately turn right up the drive till you come to a footpath sign and stile on your left. Take this across the field to the right of a large pond and out to the left-hand corner of the field. Another stile and the stream appears on your left. Follow this to the car park entrance. You will probably want to change into clean shoes before you walk left up the road to the tea rooms and a visit to Dedham.

Walk 18
BRIGHTLINGSEA

Brightlingsea is practically an island on the River Colne and has a long history of boat building, yachting and oyster farming. This walk is full of interest, following the coast to the west of the attractive town as far as Alresford Creek, with views across to Mersea Island. At the ford you turn south on higher ground, walking away from the water and enjoying the quaint old farms with crops, pigs and cattle. Join the B1029 for the mile to the Coffee Pot in the main square and after your refreshments it is only a short walk to Western Promenade and back to you car.

 The Coffee Pot, opposite the War Memorial at the west end of the High Street, serves a good selection of teas – Darjeeling, China, Indian, Earl Grey and Assam, with coffee or soft drinks as alternatives. Ploughman's, sandwiches and omelettes are available or if you are looking for lunch there is a special dish each day which can be augmented with a dessert of you choice. Opening times 8.30 am to 4.30 pm, Monday to Saturday. Telephone: 01206 305738. If the Coffee Pot is closed, there are several pubs around the central square where refreshments may be found.

DISTANCE: 6 miles.
MAP: OS Explorer 184 Colchester, Harwich and Clacton on Sea.
STARTING POINT: Western Promenade car park (GR 079163).
HOW TO GET THERE: Leave the A120 on the A133. At the first roundabout turn right for Colchester and then go left on the B1029 for Thorrington and Brightlingsea. Bear right down Station Road and on to Promenade Way. The free car park is signposted.

THE WALK

Anyone might assume that the name Brightlingsea simply shows the connection with the sea, when in reality 'sea' reminds us that the place was once an island. Long ago Brightlingsea was affiliated to Sandwich as a Cinque port member. In medieval times there was a considerable amount of shipping here but now it is best known for a flourishing yacht club and its oysters. In the High Street is Jacobes Hall, one of our oldest timbered buildings. The Beriffe family of shipping merchants bought the house from the Jacobes in about 1400, and probably inserted the great beam across a fireplace in the hall.

1. Depending on the weather and the day of the week Western Promenade may be bustling with activity or very quiet. Continue walking to the west and cross a stile on the sea wall. Keep along this for over 2 miles.

On your left the river Colne is full of interesting marine activities and beyond you will see Mersea Island, while on the mainland the countryside is peaceful, remote and sparsely farmed.

2. Turn right as you pass sand and gravel pits. Turn right on reaching Alresford Creek and come to the ford. Now turn right, southwards,

111

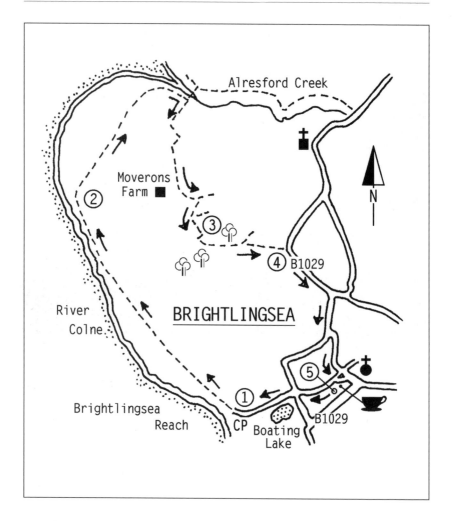

and join a wider track passing a healthy pig farm (Moverons Farm). On your right is the quaintly named Big Wapping Hill – all 60 feet of it!

3. Walk right and left along a wide track. Look for an arrow on the path and turn off the main track to the south across a field. Walk through a short thicket, cross another field, and cross a wood.

Looking across the river to Aylesford.

Continue for ½ mile to pass a sports centre to the B1029 at a corner.

4. Turn right along Church Road, then Ladysmith Avenue to the town centre and the Coffee Pot.

5. Now turn left into Station Road and join Promenade Way to regain your car.

You may wish to visit Thorrington Tide Mill nearby in Brightlingsea Road with its fully restored machinery. It is an attractive location with a public footpath along the creek. Admission free. Open the last Sunday in each month and bank holidays, March to September 2pm to 5pm. Telephone: 01621 828162.

Walk 19
WALTON ON THE NAZE

This walk must be regarded as a classic of its kind. Firstly, it is beside water most of the way. Secondly, in a distant part of Essex where we find in the height of the summer crowds of holidaymakers, at other times of year there is only the remoteness of the North Sea and the calls of the seabirds. No difficulty should be found in navigating this walk. Just follow the request – On the sea wall, water on the left! Yet with the simplicity there is satisfaction galore, particularly for bird watchers, complemented by a visit to a satisfying cafe afterwards.

☕ Just at a sharp right-hand bend in Hall Lane (No 134), the Naze Cafe provides food and drink of good quality at extremely modest prices. As, for example, battered cod and chips, steak and kidney pie and vegetables, omelettes, jacket potatoes, even home-made pasta. On Sundays a two course roast meal is served. Desserts are also home-made, changing each day and a choice of five. To drink there is tea, coffee, filter coffee, cappuccino, soft drinks and mineral water. You may also take in your own beer or wine. Opening hours are 9 am to 4 pm (Sunday 10 am to 4 pm). The Naze is closed on Wednesday but in July and August the cafe is open seven days a week 9 am to 8 pm. Telephone: 01255 679077. When the Naze Cafe is closed, refreshment can be found in any of the three pubs in the High Street.

DISTANCE: 4 miles.

MAP: OS Explorer 184 Colchester, Harwich and Clacton on Sea.

STARTING POINT: On the corner opposite the Naze Cafe (GR 259229). Street parking is available nearby in High Tree Lane or in parts of Naze Park Road.

HOW TO GET THERE: Join the A133 either from Colchester or by way of the A120. Leave the A133 on the B1033 through Weeley and Thorpe le Soken. Turn left at crossroads onto the B1034. When you reach a T-junction at Walton church turn left for a mile to come to the Naze Cafe.

ALTERNATIVE STARTING POINT: Pass the cafe and continue up Naze Park Road into Old Hall Lane. Near the Tower is a pay and display car park. Follow the directions at 5 to join the start of the walk at 1.

THE WALK

1. At the corner of Hall Lane follow a concrete public footpath sign along a well defined path with a tall hedge on your left. Soon you join a sea wall which leads to the waterside by a landing place.

2. Walk northwards to Walton Channel. The size of this channel is considerably increased by the injection of another stream called the Twizzle. Enjoy the nautical activities on the channel and the birds flying from the sea over land. You will soon reach the north-west tip of the Naze where you may pause to admire the views of Harwich and Felixstowe. All round on the wall the height has been augmented by 2 to 3 feet by concrete slabs. If this method is

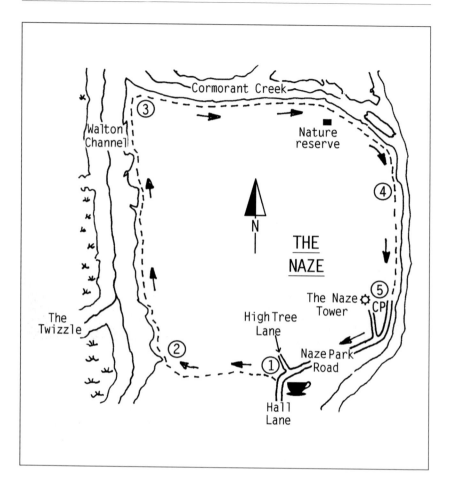

successful it must be considerably cheaper than raising the wall as in coastal defences elsewhere.

3. Turn right walking eastward along the side of Cormorant Creek. As you near the North Sea the concrete slabs are replaced by red metal girders. The walk turns to the right, the path becomes tarmacadam and passes a nature reserve owned by the Essex Wildlife Trust. The metal path ends above the beginnings of the cliffs.

Spare time to enjoy the tranquillity of the Walton channel.

These cliffs at Naze form one of the finest geographical sites in Britain so are a site of special scientific interest (SSSI). They are a prime birdwatching site. These are the birds to be spotted – lapwings, red shank, sedge and reed warblers nesting in the John Weston Reserve, as well as firecrest, red back shrike, and barred warbler, oyster catcher, curlew, gull, black headed gull, herring gull, gannets, kittiwakes, sandpipers, and cliff sand martins.

4. Take care as the cliffs have over the years slowly disintegrated and it is better to walk through the bushes for 50 yards to reach the wide sward leading up to the Walton Tower. A notice warns you to keep away from the edge. If you are lucky the refreshment stall at the Tower may be open to satisfy you needs for a drink or ice cream.

Walton is generally overshadowed by Clacton and Frinton on the eastern coast of Essex. It is, however, in its own right a fine centre for sailing and fishing with several creeks accessible to the North Sea. It also boasts a pier which is the second longest in Essex and England. The Naze is believed to be an old spelling of Nose. In the northern part of Walton a large promontory of land is bordered by water almost all the way round. An old map shows that the Naze was a large snub-nose of land 300 years ago. The Tower was built originally as a beacon, in 1720.

5. Pass the pay car park and walk in front of a row of houses facing the sea. When the gravel road turns right the path continues straight on through an uncultivated patch and in a few yards joins the Naze Park Road. Follow this back to where your car was parked, and to the teashop

Walk 20
HARWICH

A walk in two parts to discover some of the best of this historic port. The first two or so miles follow the coast south from Navyard Wharf, passing Beacon Cliff and walking the whole sweep of Dovercourt Bay. You pass no fewer than four old lighthouse beacons on the way and will be entertained by a large selection of ships and boats going into both Harwich and Felixstowe harbours. At the Groyne you head inland along the edge of the sports field to take an interesting series of 'twittens'. These town paths take you to a quiet road out to an allotment area and back to the garden of remembrance and a high path overlooking Dovercourt Bay. You now follow the main road back into town passing Redoubt Fort and the High Lighthouse on you way back to the cars and the welcoming Ship.

☕ The welcoming Ship Restaurant and Coffee Shop is opposite the Navyard Wharf in Kings Quay Street. The house specialities are without doubt the home-cooked locally caught fish. When we visited, the Over the Yard Arm menu included whitebait, Dover sole, sea bass, huss, plaice, cod, haddock, skate, herring and crab. Other main meals like steak, chicken and lasagne are available. Light meals include jacket potatoes and children's meals. In the coffee shop, there is a full range of tea, filter coffee, soft drinks, beer, cider and wine. Plus a choice of gateaux, hot puddings and ice cream. Breakfasts are available from 7 am to 10.30 am. The Ship is open from 7 am but only serves lunches from 12 noon to 4 pm Sundays and 5 pm the rest of the week. But if you are seeking cooked food the last order is one hour before closing time. Telephone: 01255 504964 to book a table. Alternative places to find refreshment include any of several pubs in the town, another teashop and a snack van sited on the quay.

DISTANCE: 5¼ miles.

MAP: OS Explorer 184 Colchester, Harwich and Clacton-on-Sea.

STARTING POINT: The public car park in Wellington Road. From the outer part of town westward, turn north-east right passing Navyard Wharf. This road leads into Wellington Road and the car park is the last entrance on the left before you turn back to the shopping centre (GR 262327). Toilets available near the High Lighthouse and along the sea front.

HOW TO GET THERE: Follow the A120T from just north-east of Colchester east into Harwich (either stay on the A120T or take the B1352 from Ramsey via Dovercourt). Head towards Harwich Harbour where you pass the Navyard Wharf to get to the car park.

ALTERNATIVE STARTING POINT: From West End free car park near the Groyne start at point 2 (GR 246300).

THE WALK

In the 12th century Harwich was a walled town defended by a castle. Medieval Harwich was an early example of town planning on the grid iron pattern. Many of the houses were refronted in Georgian times, and cellars were interconnecting which aided smuggling and enabled many a poor

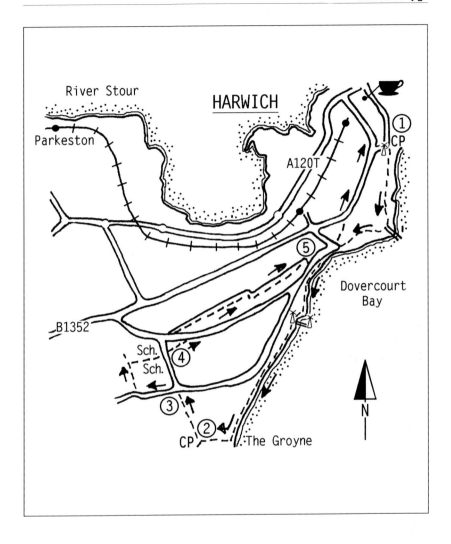

wretch to escape the press gangs. Harwich has the oldest unaltered purpose-built cinema in Britain built in 1911. The Treadwheel Crane was built in the mid 1660s and moved here for visitors to see. The Low Lighthouse houses a museum of specialised displays of Royal Navy and commercial shipping. HMS Ganges is well represented as are plans of boats going back to the good old days of sail. The highlight could be to climb up inside the *lighthouse and then walk around its light. Pick a calm sunny day and you are in for a treat.*

1. From the car park climb onto the sea wall, turn right and follow the promenade southwards for just over 2 miles. You will pass the Treadwheel Crane, the Low Lighthouse and walk round Beacon Cliff and pass Beacon Hill Fort. You may feel a little exposed for two or three steps as you pass the breakwater. The sweep of Dovercourt Bay takes you past two further lighthouses. The Groyne with its large selection of beach huts marks the end of this waterside walk.

Dovercourt Bay has been a fine holiday resort since the 1850s. You will find good toilet facilities, breakwaters to enable bathing and for 'those in the know' a host of beach huts. The statue of Queen Victoria proudly dominates the whole bay.

2. Near beach hut number 258 you will find you are opposite West End free car park. Turn right and pass the Civic Amenity Site, then walk along the edge of the sports field on the grass if it is safer to do so. You soon come to crossroads and a footpath sign.

3. Turn left and when it is safe to do so cross the road. Walk along for about ¼ mile till you come to the 22B and 103 bus stop. Just past this you will find a footpath sign, turn right and walk with a school playing field on your right. Then 36 paces past a pillbox turn right and walk between the two schools out to the road.

4. Turn left, cross the road and then walk right by the 103 footpath sign. This short twitten soon brings you to another footpath sign and road. Turn left towards the water tower and immediately right on a narrow back road where in places cars are banned. Basically you cross four crossing roads but still continue walking in the same direction on this back road. Old Vicarage Road and the allotments appear on you right. Keep rightish into a small uphill climb on Elmshurst Road.

5. At the T-junction turn left. You may like to find an ice cream at the

The Harwich Redoubt Fort enjoys a commanding view over Harwich harbour.

convenience store as you pass on your way to the garden of remembrance. There are now good views of the bay as you walk down Marine Parade. As the road goes left walk straight on and pass a white gate. The park is in front of you. Take the path leftish marked Redoubt. Cross Barrack Lane and head along Main Road towards the High Lighthouse. You pass the Redoubt Fort.

The Redoubt Fort is behind 29 Main Road up a very steep climb. This circular building was built with a commanding view over Harwich Harbour in 1808–1810 to defend Harwich from Napoleon. It is open daily in the summer and is well worth a visit. The High Lighthouse is a 90 foot nine-sided tower built in 1818 that became redundant in 1863. In more recent years it has become famous for marking the end of the Essex Way long distance walking route that starts at Epping.

At the lighthouse make your way to the sea front and the cars. Make your way north back the way you drove along Wellington Road to Kings Quay Street and refreshments at the Ship opposite Navyard Wharf.